IN THE SHADOW'S LIGHT

CE QUI FUT SANS LUMIÈRE

Yves Bonnefoy

IN THE SHADOW'S LIGHT

Yves Bonnefoy

TRANSLATED BY

John Naughton

WITH AN INTERVIEW WITH

YVES BONNEFOY

THE UNIVERSITY OF CHICAGO PRESS

Chicago & London

YVES BONNEFOY, professor of comparative poetics at the Collège de
France in Paris, is widely considered the most important and influential
French poet since World War II. His five earlier books of poetry have
been translated into English. He received the Prix Goncourt for poetry
in 1987 and the Bennett Award in 1988.

THE UNIVERSITY OF CHICAGO PRESS, CHICAGO 60637
THE UNIVERSITY OF CHICAGO PRESS, LTD., LONDON
© 1991 by The University of Chicago
All rights reserved. Published 1991
Printed in the United States of America
00 99 98 97 96 95 94 93 92 91   5 4 3 2 1

Originally published as *Ce qui fut sans lumière,* by Yves Bonnefoy. Paris:
Mercure de France, 1987. © 1987.

Library of Congress Cataloging-in-Publication Data

Bonnefoy, Yves.
[Ce qui fut sans lumière. English & French]
In the shadow's light / Yves Bonnefoy ; translated by John
Naughton ; with an interview with Yves Bonnefoy.
    p.   cm.
English and French.
ISBN 0-226-06447-6
I. Title.
PQ2603.O533C413   1991
821'.914—dc20   90-38229
                                                    CIP

∞ The paper used in this publication meets
the minimum requirements of the American National
Standard for Information Sciences—Permanence of
Paper for Printed Library Materials, ANSI Z39.48–1984.
This book is printed on acid-free paper.

For as well the pillar of *cloud* as that of *fire* . . .

John Donne

Contents

Translator's Note

Ce qui fut sans lumière (*In the Shadow's Light*), published in 1987, is Yves Bonnefoy's fifth major book of poetry. Like all of his poetical work, this volume is organized around the principle of death and resurrection, disappointment and resurgent hope, farewell and new departure. A central place is given to the evocation of the abandoned monastery in Provence which Bonnefoy acquired in the early 1960s and in which he spent some of the deepest and richest moments of his life. The sense of leaving this place, of turning toward the unknown, mingles with memories of the past, and of early childhood. The poet manages to translate the painful sense of loss into a confidence in the unforeseen, and to create from the strains of dispossession an autumnal register that is as haunting as anything he has ever written. The poet discusses his work in some detail in an interview he gave in October 1989. This interview appears in the present volume after the text of the poems.

I

Le Souvenir

Ce souvenir me hante, que le vent tourne
D'un coup, là-bas, sur la maison fermée.
C'est un grand bruit de toile par le monde,
On dirait que l'étoffe de la couleur
Vient de se déchirer jusqu'au fond des choses.
Le souvenir s'éloigne mais il revient,
C'est un homme et une femme masqués, on dirait qu'ils tentent
De mettre à flot une barque trop grande.
Le vent rabat la voile sur leurs gestes,
Le feu prend dans la voile, l'eau est noire,
Que faire de tes dons, ô souvenir,

Sinon recommencer le plus vieux rêve,
Croire que je m'éveille? La nuit est calme,
Sa lumière ruisselle sur les eaux,
La voile des étoiles frémit à peine
Dans la brise qui passe par les mondes.
La barque de chaque chose, de chaque vie
Dort, dans la masse de l'ombre de la terre,

Et la maison respire, presque sans bruit,
L'oiseau dont nous ne savions pas le nom dans la vallée
À peine a-t-il lancé, on dirait moqueuses
Mais non sans compassion, ce qui fait peur,
Ses deux notes presque indistinctes trop près de nous.
Je me lève, j'écoute ce silence,
Je vais à la fenêtre, une fois encore,
Qui domine la terre que j'ai aimée.
Ô joies, comme un rameur au loin, qui bouge peu
Sur la nappe brillante; et plus loin encore
Brûlent sans bruit terrestre les flambeaux
Des montagnes, des fleuves, des vallées.
Joies, et nous ne savions si c'était en nous

The Memory

I am haunted by this memory, that the wind
All at once is swirling over the closed up house.
There is a mighty sound of flapping sail throughout the world,
As if the stuff that color is made of
Had just been rent to the very depths of things.
The memory passes, then returns,
It is a man and a woman who are masked, they seem
To be trying to push a boat that is too big into water.
The wind thrashes the sail on their arms and hands,
Fire catches in the sail, the water is black,
What can I make of your gifts, O memory,

If not begin once more the oldest dream,
Believe that I am waking? The night is calm,
Its light is streaming on the waters,
The sail of the stars is scarcely stirring
In the breeze passing through the worlds.
The bark of each thing, of each life
Is sleeping in earth's heavy mass of shadow,

And the house is breathing, almost soundlessly,
The bird in the valley, the one we could not name,
Has faintly thrown out, too close to us,
Its two almost indistinct notes that seem mocking,
And yet not without compassion, which is frightening.
I get up, I listen to this silence,
Once again I go to the window
That looks out over the country I have loved.
O joys, like an oarsman in the distance, barely
Moving on the bright expanse; and further still
The torches of the mountains, the rivers, the valleys
Are burning, far from any earthly sound.
Joys—and we never knew if it was in us,

Comme vaine rumeur et lueur de rêve
Cette suite de salles et de tables
Chargées de fruits, de pierres et de fleurs,
Ou ce qu'un dieu voulait, pour une fête
Qu'il donnerait, puisque nous consentions,
Tout un été dans sa maison d'enfance.

Joies, et le temps qui vint au travers, comme un fleuve
En crue, de nuit, débouche dans le rêve
Et en blesse la rive, et en disperse
Les images les plus sereines dans la boue.
Je ne veux pas savoir la question qui monte
De cette terre en paix, je me détourne,
Je traverse les chambres de l'étage
Où dort toute une part de ce que je fus,
Je descends dans la nuit des arches d'en bas
Vers le feu qui végète dans l'église,
Je me penche sur lui, qui bouge d'un coup
Comme un dormeur que l'on touche à l'épaule
Et se redresse un peu, levant vers moi
L'épiphanie de sa face de braise.
Non, plutôt rendors-toi, feu éternel,
Tire sur toi la cape de tes cendres,
Réacquiesce à ton rêve, puisque tu bois
Toi aussi à la coupe de l'or rapide.
L'heure n'est pas venue de porter la flamme
Dans le miroir qui nous parle dans l'ombre,
J'ai à demeurer seul. J'ouvre la porte
Qui donne sur les amandiers dont rien ne bouge,
Si paisible est la nuit qui les vêt de lune.

Et j'avance, dans l'herbe froide. Ô terre, terre,
Présence si consentante, si donnée,
Est-il vrai que déjà nous ayons vécu
L'heure où l'on voit s'éteindre, de branche en branche,
Les guirlandes du soir de fête? Et on ne sait,

4

Like idle murmurings and the glowing of dream,
This succession of rooms and of tables
Laden with fruit, with stones and with flowers,
Or if it was what some god, seeing how
Willing we were, had wanted to prepare
For a summer's celebration in his childhood home.

Joys, and time that passed through, like a river
Rising at night, flows into the dream
And wounds its shore and scatters
Its most peaceful images in the mud.
I do not want to know the question rising
From this tranquil earth, I turn away,
I cross the rooms of the upper floor
Where much of what I was is still asleep,
I go down into the night of the arches below
Toward the fire languishing in the church,
I lean over it, and it stirs suddenly,
Like someone sleeping who is touched on the shoulder,
Then rises a little, lifting towards me
The epiphany of its ember face.
No, rather return to sleep, eternal fire,
Draw your cape of ashes over yourself,
Go back to your dream, since you too
Drink from the cup of fast flowing gold.
The hour has not yet come to carry the flame
Into the mirror that speaks to us in shadow.
I must remain alone. I open the door that
Leads out to the almond trees, whose branches do not move,
So still is the night that clothes them in moon.

And I go forward, into the cold grasses. O earth, earth,
Presence so compliant, so fully offered,
Can it be that already we have lived
The moment when one sees, from branch to branch,
The garlands of our joyful evenings die out?

Seuls à nouveau dans la nuit qui s'achève,
Si même on veut que reparaisse l'aube
Tant le cœur reste pris à ces voix qui chantent
Là-bas, encore, et se font indistinctes
En s'éloignant sur les chemins de sable.

Je vais
Le long de la maison vers le ravin, je vois
Vaguement miroiter les choses du simple
Comme un chemin qui s'ouvre, sous l'étoile
Qui prépare le jour. Terre, est-il vrai
Que tant de sève dans l'amandier au mois des fleurs,
Tant de feux dans le ciel, tant de rayons
Dès l'aube dans les vitres, dans le miroir,
Tant d'ignorances dans nos vies mais tant d'espoirs,
Tant de désir de toi, terre parfaite,
N'étaient pas faits pour mûrir comme un fruit
En son instant d'extase se détache
De la branche, de la matière, saveur pure?

Je vais,
Et il me semble que quelqu'un marche près de moi,
Ombre, qui sourirait bien que silencieuse
Comme une jeune fille, pieds nus dans l'herbe,
Accompagne un instant celui qui part.
Et celui-ci s'arrête, il la regarde,
Il prendrait volontiers dans ses mains ce visage
Qui est la terre même. Adieu, dit-il,
Présence qui ne fut que pressentie
Bien que mystérieusement tant d'années si proche,
Adieu, image impénétrable qui nous leurra
D'être la vérité enfin presque dite,
Certitude, là où tout n'a été que doute, et bien que chimère
Parole si ardente que réelle.
Adieu, nous ne te verrons plus venir près de nous

And, alone once more in the night that draws to an end,
One wonders if one even wants dawn to reappear,
So strongly is the heart drawn to those voices
That are singing over there, still, and grow dim
As they fade away on the paths of sand.

I pass along
The side of the house toward the ravine, I can see
The simple earthly things shimmering faintly,
Like a road opening up, beneath the star
That prepares for day. Earth, can it be
That so much sap in the almond tree
The month of its flowering,
That so many fires in the sky, so much light at dawn
On the windowpanes, on the mirror,
That so much ignorance in our lives, but also so much hope,
So much desire for you, O perfect earth,
That all this was not made to ripen like the fruit,
In its moment of ecstasy, when it breaks away
From the branch, from matter, as pure savor?

I go on,
And it seems to me that someone is walking beside me,
A shade that seems to smile, and yet is silent,
Like a young girl, barefoot in the grass,
Who walks for awhile with someone who is leaving.
He stops and looks at her,
He would gladly take this face in his hands,
This face that is the earth itself. Farewell, he whispers,
Farewell, presence that was but dimly sensed,
Although for so many years so mysteriously close,
Farewell, unfathomable image that beguiled us
All the more as it was the truth almost spoken,
Certainty, when everything else was only doubt, and though
But a dream, speech so ardent it was real.
Farewell, no longer shall we see you come near us

Avec l'offrande du ciel et des feuilles sèches,
Nous ne te verrons pas rapprocher de l'âtre
Tout ton profil de servante divine.
Adieu, nous n'étions pas de même destin,
Tu as à prendre ce chemin et nous cet autre,
Et entre s'épaissit cette vallée
Que l'inconnu surplombe
Avec un cri rapide d'oiseau qui chasse.
Adieu, tu es déjà touchée par d'autres lèvres,
L'eau du fleuve n'appartient pas à son rivage
Sauf par le grand bruit clair.
J'envie le dieu du soir qui se penchera
Sur le vieillissement de ta lumière.
Terre, ce qu'on appelle la poésie
T'aura tant désirée en ce siècle, sans prendre
Jamais sur toi le bien du geste d'amour!

Il l'a touchée de ses mains, de ses lèvres,
Il la retient, qui sourit, par la nuque,
Il la regarde, en ces yeux qui s'effacent
Dans la phosphorescence de ce qui est.
Et maintenant, enfin, il se détourne.
Je le vois qui s'éloigne dans la nuit.

Adieu? Non, ce n'est pas le mot que je sais dire.

Et mes rêves, serrés
L'un contre l'autre et l'autre encore, ainsi
La sortie des brebis dans le premier givre,
Reprennent piétinant leurs plus vieux chemins.
Je m'éveille nuit après nuit dans la maison vide,
Il me semble qu'un pas m'y précède encore.
Je sors
Et m'étonne que l'ampoule soit allumée
Dans ce lieu déserté de tous, devant l'étable.

With your offerings of sky and dry leaves,
No longer shall we see you bring toward the hearth
That profile of servant divine.
Farewell, our destinies were not the same,
You must take this path and we this other,
And between them grows deeper and denser
That valley which the unknown looms over
With the quick cry of the swooping bird of prey.
Farewell, already other lips are touching you,
The water of the river leaves to its banks
Only its great clear sound.
I envy the god of evening who will bend over
Your aging light.
Earth, what we call poetry
Will have felt, in this century, such desire for you,
Without ever taking upon you the blessings
Of the act of love!

He has touched her with his hands, his lips,
He holds her, she is smiling, by the neck,
He looks at her, in those eyes that disappear
Into the phosphorescence of what is.
And now, at last, he turns away.
I can see him going off into the night.

Farewell? No, this is not the word I can say.

And my dreams, pressed
One against another, and still another, like
Sheep that venture into the first frost,
Trample once more onto their old, familiar paths.
I wake up, night after night, in the empty house,
I still hear the sound of footsteps ahead of me.
I go out
And am surprised to see the light bulb burning
On the wall of the now deserted stable.

Je cours derrière la maison, parce que l'appel
Du berger d'autrefois retentit encore.
J'entends l'aboi qui précédait le jour,
Je vois l'étoile boire parmi les bêtes
Qui ne sont plus, à l'aube. Et résonne encore la flûte
Dans la fumée des choses transparentes.

I run behind the house, because the shepherd's call
From times gone by is still resounding.
I hear the barking that announced daybreak,
I can see the star drinking at dawn
Amid the flocks that are no longer.
And in the smoke of things transparent,
The sounds of the flute are still echoing.

Attracted by your divinity and so tickled
by this poison soil Unguarded from your
flesh and plays of mankind Misleading
theatre

Les Arbres

Nous regardions nos arbres, c'était du haut
De la terrasse qui nous fut chère, le soleil
Se tenait près de nous cette fois encore
Mais en retrait, hôte silencieux
Au seuil de la maison en ruines, que nous laissions
À son pouvoir, immense, illuminée.

Vois, te disais-je, il fait glisser contre la pierre
Inégale, incompréhensible, de notre appui
L'ombre de nos épaules confondues,
Celle des amandiers qui sont près de nous
Et celle même du haut des murs qui se mêle aux autres,
Trouée, barque brûlée, proue qui dérive,
Comme un surcroît de rêve ou de fumée.

Mais ces chênes là-bas sont immobiles,
Même leur ombre ne bouge pas, dans la lumière,
Ce sont les rives du temps qui coule ici où nous sommes,
Et leur sol est inabordable, tant est rapide
Le courant de l'espoir gros de la mort.

Nous regardâmes les arbres toute une heure.
Le soleil attendait, parmi les pierres,
Puis il eut compassion, il étendit
Vers eux, en contrebas dans le ravin,
Nos ombres qui parurent les atteindre
Comme, avançant le bras, on peut toucher
Parfois, dans la distance entre deux êtres,
Un instant du rêve de l'autre, qui va sans fin.

The Trees

We were looking at our trees from up
On the terrace we loved, the sun
Lingered near us this time as well,
But at a certain distance, a silent guest
In the doorway of the house in ruins,
Which we had left full of light to his power.

Look, I told you, he slides against the uneven,
Incomprehensible stone we lean upon
The shadow cast by our mingling shoulders,
And the one made by the almond trees close by;
And even the shadow of the tops of the walls that blends
With the others, riddled with holes, charred bark,
Drifting prow, like a surfeit of dream or smoke.

But the oak trees down there are motionless,
Even their shadow does not move, in the light,
These are the shores of Time, that flows
Here where we are,
And on this ground no one can land,
So fast is the current of hope pregnant with death.

For a whole hour we looked at the trees.
The sun tarried, among the stones,
Then felt compassion and stretched out
Towards them, down below in the ravine,
Our shadows, and they seemed to meet,
Just as, reaching out an arm, one can sometimes
Touch, in the distance between two people,
A moment of another person's endless dream.

L'Épervier

Il y a nombre d'années,
À V.,
Nous avons vu le temps venir au-devant de nous
Qui regardions par la fenêtre ouverte
De la chambre au-dessus de la chapelle.
C'était un épervier
Qui regagnait son nid au creux du mur.
Il tenait dans son bec un serpent mort.
Quand il nous vit
Il cria de colère et d'angoisse pure
Mais sans lâcher sa proie et, immobile
Dans la lumière de l'aube,
Il forma avec elle le signe même
Du début, du milieu et de la fin.

Et il y avait là
Dans le pays d'été, très près du ciel,
Nombre de vases, serrés; et de chacun
S'élevait une flamme; et de chaque flamme
La couleur était autre, qui bruissait,
Vapeur ou rêve, ou monde, sous l'étoile.
On eût dit d'un affairement d'âmes, attendues
À un appontement au bout d'une île.
Je croyais même entendre des mots, ou presque
(Presque, soit par défaut, soit par excès
De la puissance infirme du langage),
Passer, comme un frémissement de la chaleur
Dans l'air phosphorescent qui ne faisait qu'une
De toutes ces couleurs dont il me semblait
Que certaines, au loin, m'étaient inconnues.

Je les touchais, elles ne brûlaient pas.
J'y avançais la main, non, je ne prenais rien
De ces grappes d'un autre fruit que la lumière.

The Sparrow-Hawk

Many years ago,
At V.,
We saw time come to meet us
As we watched from the open window
Of the room above the chapel.
It was a sparrow-hawk
Flying back to his nest in the hollow of the wall.
In his beak he held a dead snake.
When he saw us,
He cried out in anger and in pure anguish,
But without letting his prey fall,
And, motionless in the light of dawn,
He formed with it the very sign
Of the beginning, the middle, and the end.

And there,
In the land of summer, very near the sky,
A number of vases stood close to one another;
And from each a flame rose up; and the color
Of each flame was different, and it rustled,
Vapor or dream, or world, beneath the star.
We might have thought it was the bustling of souls
Expected at a pier at the end of an island.
I even thought I had heard words, produced
By what is either lacking or nascent
In the crippled power of our language,
Invade, like a quiver of the summer's heat,
The phosphorescent air that turned into one
All these colors, some of which seemed,
The most distant, quite unknown to me.

I touched them, they were not burning.
I extended my hand, no, I took nothing
From these clusters of another fruit than light.

L'Adieu

Nous sommes revenus à notre origine.
Ce fut le lieu de l'évidence, mais déchirée.
Les fenêtres mêlaient trop de lumières,
Les escaliers gravissaient trop d'étoiles
Qui sont des arches qui s'effondrent, des gravats,
Le feu semblait brûler dans un autre monde.

Et maintenant des oiseaux volent de chambre en chambre,
Les volets sont tombés, le lit est couvert de pierres,
L'âtre plein de débris du ciel qui vont s'éteindre.
Là nous parlions, le soir, presque à voix basse
À cause des rumeurs des voûtes, là pourtant
Nous formions nos projets: mais une barque,
Chargée de pierres rouges, s'éloignait
Irrésistiblement d'une rive, et l'oubli
Posait déjà sa cendre sur les rêves
Que nous recommencions sans fin, peuplant d'images
Le feu qui a brûlé jusqu'au dernier jour.

Est-il vrai, mon amie,
Qu'il n'y a qu'un seul mot pour désigner
Dans la langue qu'on nomme la poésie
Le soleil du matin et celui du soir,
Un seul le cri de joie et le cri d'angoisse,
Un seul l'amont désert et les coups de haches,
Un seul le lit défait et le ciel d'orage,
Un seul l'enfant qui naît et le dieu mort?

Oui, je le crois, je veux le croire, mais quelles sont
Ces ombres qui emportent le miroir?
Et vois, la ronce prend parmi les pierres
Sur la voie d'herbe encore mal frayée
Où se portaient nos pas vers les jeunes arbres.

The Farewell

We have come back to our origin.
The place where all had been evident, now torn.
The windows mingled too many lights,
The stairs climbed too many stars
Which are collapsing arches, rubble;
The fire seemed to burn in another world.

And now birds fly from room to room,
The shutters have come down, the bed is covered with stones,
The fireplace full of the sky's dying debris.
It was here that we would talk at evening, almost in whispers,
Because of the echoing from the vaulted ceiling, here that
We would make our plans: but a boat,
Loaded with red stones, moved away,
Irresistibly, from a shore, and oblivion
Was already placing its ashes on the dreams
That we endlessly renewed, peopling with images
The fire that burned until the last morning.

Beloved, is it true
That in the language called poetry
There is only one word for designating
The morning and the evening sun,
One word for the cry of joy and the cry of anguish,
One for the woods upstream and the falling ax,
One for the unmade bed and the stormy sky,
One for the newborn child and the god who died?

Yes, I think so, I want to think so, but who are
These shades that are carrying off the mirror?
And look, brambles are springing up among the stones
Along the barely beaten path through the grasses
That took us out toward the young trees.

Il me semble aujourd'hui, ici, que la parole
Est cette auge à demi brisée, dont se répand
À chaque aube de pluie l'eau inutile.

L'herbe et dans l'herbe l'eau qui brille, comme un fleuve.
Tout est toujours à remailler du monde.
Le paradis est épars, je le sais,
C'est la tâche terrestre d'en reconnaître
Les fleurs disséminées dans l'herbe pauvre,
Mais l'ange a disparu, une lumière
Qui ne fut plus soudain que soleil couchant.

Et comme Adam et Ève nous marcherons
Une dernière fois dans le jardin.
Comme Adam le premier regret, comme Ève le premier
Courage nous voudrons et ne voudrons pas
Franchir la porte basse qui s'entrouvre
Là-bas, à l'autre bout des longes, colorée
Comme auguralement d'un dernier rayon.
L'avenir se prend-il dans l'origine
Comme le ciel consent à un miroir courbe,
Pourrons-nous recueillir de cette lumière
Qui a été le miracle d'ici
La semence dans nos mains sombres, pour d'autres flaques
Au secret d'autres champs « barrés de pierres »?

Certes, le lieu pour vaincre, pour nous vaincre, c'est ici
Dont nous partons, ce soir. Ici sans fin
Comme cette eau qui s'échappe de l'auge.

It seems to me today, here, that speech
Is that half-broken trough flowing
At every rainy dawn with useless water.

The grass, and in the grass the water shimmering,
Like a river.
The work of mending in this world never ends.
Paradise lies scattered, this I know,
It is our earthly task to recognize
Its flowers that are strewn in the humble grass;
But the angel has disappeared, a light
That suddenly was but a setting sun.

And like Adam and Eve we will walk
One last time in the garden.
Like Adam the first regret, like Eve the first
Courage, we will want and not want
To pass through the low, half-opened door
Down there, at the other end of the field, colored
As though prophetically with a last ray of light.
Will the future spring from the origin
As the sky gives itself to a convex mirror?
From that light which has been the miracle
Of here and now, will we gather up
In darker hands the seeds for other pools of water
Hidden in other fields "among the stones"?

Surely the place of victory, of victory over ourselves,
Is here in what we are leaving tonight. Endlessly here
Like that water overflowing from the trough.

Le Miroir courbe

Regarde-les là-bas, à ce carrefour,
Qui semblent hésiter puis qui repartent.
L'enfant court devant eux, ils ont cueilli
En de grandes brassées pour les quelques vases
Ces fleurs d'à travers champs qui n'ont pas de nom.

Et l'ange est au-dessus, qui les observe
Enveloppé du vent de ses couleurs.
Un de ses bras est nu dans l'étoffe rouge,
On dirait qu'il tient un miroir, et que la terre
Se reflète dans l'eau de cette autre rive.

Et que désigne-t-il maintenant, du doigt
Qui pointe vers un lieu dans cette image?
Est-ce une autre maison ou un autre monde,
Est-ce même une porte, dans la lumière
Ici mêlée des choses et des signes?

The Convex Mirror

I

Look at them down there, at that crossroads,
They seem to hesitate, then go on.
The child runs before them, they have picked
By the armful, for their few vases,
Those field flowers that have no name.

And the angel is above, watching them,
Enveloped in the wind of his colors.
One bare arm in the red cloth,
He seems to be holding a mirror, the earth
Reflected in the water of this other shore.

And what is he showing now with his finger
That is pointing toward a place in the image?
Is it some other house or some other world,
Is it even a door,
Among these things and signs now a single light?

II

Ils aiment rentrer tard, ainsi. Ils ne distinguent
Plus même le chemin parmi les pierres
D'où sourd encore une ombre d'ocre rouge.
Ils ont pourtant confiance. Près du seuil
L'herbe est facile et il n'est point de mort.

Et les voici maintenant sous des voûtes.
Il y fait noir dans la rumeur des feuilles
Sèches, que fait bouger sur le dallage
Le vent qui ne sait pas, de salle en salle,
Ce qui a nom et ce qui n'est que chose.

Ils vont, ils vont. Là-bas parmi les ruines,
C'est le pays où les rives sont calmes,
Les chemins immobiles. Dans les chambres
Ils placeront les fleurs, près du miroir
Qui peut-être consume, et peut-être sauve.

II

They like to come in late like this. They cannot even
Make out the pathway that runs through the stones
Still welling with red and ochre shadow.
But they are not afraid. Near the doorway
The grass is easy and there is no death.

And here they are now beneath the vaulted ceilings.
It is pitch black and the dry leaves are stirring
On the flagstones, blown by the wind that never knows,
As it moves from room to room,
Which things have names and which are only things.

On, on they go. Down there among the ruins
Is the land where the shores are calm,
The paths motionless. They will put the flowers
In the rooms, near the mirror
That perhaps will consume and perhaps save.

Une pierre

L'été passa violent dans les salles fraîches,
Ses yeux étaient aveugles, son flanc nu,
Il cria, et l'appel bouleversa le songe
De ceux qui dormaient là au simple de leur jour.

Ils frémirent. Changea le rythme de leur souffle,
Reposèrent leurs mains la coupe du sommeil.
Déjà le ciel venait à nouveau sur terre,
Ce fut l'orage des après-midi d'été, dans l'éternel.

A Stone

Summer passed through the cool rooms, violent,
Its eyes blind, its flanks bare;
It cried out, and its call troubled the dreams
Of those sleeping there in the simplicity of their light.

They shuddered and the rhythm of their breathing changed.
Their hands put down the heavy cup of sleep.
And already the sky was again on the earth,
Bringing the afternoon storms of summer, in the eternal.

La Voix, qui a repris

« Es-tu venu par besoin de ce lieu,
De ce lieu seul, ravin, porte dressée
Au-dessus du levant et du couchant
Comme passe la barque d'un autre monde,
Entre, je te permets presque une halte.

Es-tu venu pour, au moins une fois,
Être maître du seuil, pousser le poids
De la porte cloutée sur ses gonds qui dorment,
Et déranger ce rêve, bien que sachant
Que tout seuil est un rêve, et que ce fer
Y est certes le signe, mais sans promesse,
Je te permets la clef dans la lourde porte.

Es-tu venu pour entendre l'écho
Des marteaux sous les voûtes, mais déjà
T'éloignant, te décolorant, ne percevant
La lumière qu'en rêve, descendant
Les yeux emplis de larmes vers le ciel
Qui t'accueillait de terrasse en terrasse
Parmi les amandiers et les chênes clairs,
Vois, je t'aurai donné, en la reprenant,
Une terre natale, et il n'est rien d'autre. »

The Voice, Rising Up Once More

"Did you come out of need for this place,
This place alone, with its ravine, its door
Set above the rising and the setting sun
Like the passing bark of another world?
Enter, I will almost grant you a moment's pause.

Did you come to be, at least once,
The master of the threshold and to push open,
On its sleeping hinges, the bulk of the studded door,
And to trouble this dream, although you know
That every threshold is a dream, and this iron
Surely a sign, though it carries no promise?
Come, I will grant you the key for the heavy door.

Did you come to hear the echoing
Of the hammers beneath the roofs, but already
Withdrawing, becoming shadow, seeing
The light only in dream, going down,
Your eyes full of tears, toward the sky
That welcomed you on every terrace
Among the almond trees and the white oaks,
Look now: taking it back, I will have given you
A native earth, and there is nothing else."

La Voix encore

« Et venais-tu pour la nuque ployée
Là-haut, dans cette chambre, non, dans le ciel
D'orage, et cette main dans la tienne, et le cri
D'espoir, de joie, puis relever les yeux
Vers la cime parfaite des montagnes
Et contempler, comme nuptialement,
La beauté, qui semble augurale, de ce monde
(Car c'est là, sous l'étoile, que je demeure,
Ma parole est ce givre sous ce silence,
Le seuil est là, où la grappe des pierres
Mûrit hors de l'espace, illuminée),
—Je t'ai permis de boire à cette lumière,
Je t'ai donné l'enfant qui me désigne.

Par la brièveté de la porte, vois
Le pain brûler sur la table.
Par le bois cloué mort dans la porte, prends
Mesure de la nuit qui couvre la terre.
Par le déchirement de la couleur,
Par le gémissement des gonds de la porte, sens
Se déjointer dans l'énigme du temps
L'être de la présence et de la promesse.
La nuit est prompte et lourde à retomber
Sur le bleu du dehors du monde, dont la voix
Va te sembler trompeuse, te faire mal,
Et le cri de la nuit est âcre dans l'huile
Des gonds de toute chose: cependant,
Le poids même du fer sur la pierre témoigne
De corps suants, courbés
Sur le bâtir mystérieux et le sens.

Again the Voice

"Did you come for the bent neck
Up there in the bedroom, no, in the stormy
Sky, and for that hand in your hand, and for
The cry of hope, and joy, and then to raise
Your eyes toward the perfect mountain tops
And to gaze on the bridal beauty of this world
Which seems a beginning and a promise
(For it is there, beneath the star, that I reside,
My voice is this frost beneath this silence,
The threshold is there where the clusters of stones
Ripen outside space, illuminated)?
—I allowed you to drink from this light,
I gave you the child who points to me.

Through the briefness of the door,
See the bread burning on the table.
Through the wood nailed dead in the door,
Take stock of the night covering the earth.
Through the rending of color,
Through the groaning of the door hinges, feel
The being of presence and of promise
Come apart in the enigma of passing time.
Quickly and heavily does night
Fall upon the blue of the outer world, whose voice
Will seem deceitful to you and will wound you!
And the cry of night is bitter in the oily
Hinges of all things: and yet,
The very weight of the iron on the stone speaks of
Sweating bodies, bent over
The mystery of making and of meaning.

Et vois, la pierre
A des mots infinis dans l'herbe du seuil,
Et là, dans la chaleur,
Ce qui n'a pas de paix est la paix encore. »

And look, the stone
In the grass of the threshold has boundless words,
And there, in the heat,
What knows no peace, is peace nonetheless."

II

Passant auprès du feu

Je passais près du feu dans la salle vide
Aux volets clos, aux lumières éteintes,

Et je vis qu'il brûlait encore, et qu'il était même
En cet instant à ce point d'équilibre
Entre les forces de la cendre, de la braise
Où la flamme va pouvoir être, à son désir,
Soit violente soit douce dans l'étreinte
De qui elle a séduit sur cette couche
Des herbes odorantes et du bois mort.
Lui, c'est cet angle de la branche que j'ai rentrée
Hier, dans la pluie d'été soudain si vive,
Il ressemble à un dieu de l'Inde qui regarde
Avec la gravité d'un premier amour
Celle qui veut de lui que l'enveloppe
La foudre qui précède l'univers.

Demain je remuerai
La flamme presque froide, et ce sera
Sans doute un jour d'été comme le ciel
En a pour tous les fleuves, ceux du monde
Et ceux, sombres, du sang. L'homme, la femme,
Quand savent-ils, à temps,
Que leur ardeur se noue ou se dénoue?
Quelle sagesse en eux peut pressentir
Dans une hésitation de la lumière
Que le cri de bonheur se fait cri d'angoisse?

Feu des matins,
Respiration de deux êtres qui dorment,
Le bras de l'un sur l'épaule de l'autre.

Passing by the Fire

In the empty room, with its shutters closed,
And its lights spent, I passed by the fire.

And I saw that it still burned, that it was even,
At that moment, poised between
The powers of ash and of ember,
When the flame can choose to be
Either raging or subdued in the arms
Of what it has seduced on its bed
Of fragrant grasses and dead wood.
He is the jagged piece of branch I brought in
Yesterday, in the summer rain falling suddenly so hard.
He seems one of the gods of India, watching
With all the gravity of a first love
The one who asks of him that she be wrapped
In the lightning from before the worlds.

Tomorrow I will stir
The nearly cold flame, and doubtless
It will be a summer day like those
The sky offers to all the rivers, those of earth
And those, darker ones, of blood. Man and woman,
When do they ever know
That their passion is binding or coming apart?
What wisdom in their hearts could ever sense
That, as the light flickers,
Their cry of joy becomes a cry of anguish?

Morning fire,
The breathing of two people asleep,
The arm of one on the shoulder of the other.

Et moi qui suis venu
Ouvrir la salle, accueillir la lumière,
Je m'arrête, je m'assieds là, je vous regarde,
Innocence des membres détendus,
Temps si riche de soi qu'il a cessé d'être.

And I who came
To open the room, let in the light,
I stop, I sit there, I watch you,
Innocence of the sprawling limbs,
Time so full it ceases to be.

Le Puits

Tu écoutes la chaîne heurter la paroi
Quand le seau descend dans le puits qui est l'autre étoile,
Parfois l'étoile du soir, celle qui vient seule,
Parfois le feu sans rayons qui attend à l'aube
Que le berger et les bêtes sortent.

Mais toujours l'eau est close, au fond du puits,
Toujours l'étoile y demeure scellée.
On y perçoit des ombres, sous des branches,
Ce sont des voyageurs qui passent de nuit

Courbés, le dos chargé d'une masse noire,
Hésitant, dirait-on, à un carrefour.
Certains semblent attendre, d'autres s'effacent
Dans l'étincellement qui va sans lumière.

Le voyage de l'homme, de la femme est long, plus long
   que la vie,
C'est une étoile au bout du chemin, un ciel
Qu'on a cru voir briller entre deux arbres.
Quand le seau touche l'eau, qui le soulève,
C'est une joie puis la chaîne l'accable.

The Well

You hear the chain striking the wall
When the bucket goes down into the well, that other star,
Sometimes the evening star, the one that comes alone,
Sometimes the fire without rays that waits at dawn
For the shepherd and his flock to go out.

But the water at the bottom of the well is always closed,
And the star there remains forever sealed.
You can see shadows there, beneath branches,
That are travelers passing by night

Bowed down beneath a load of blackness they go
As if hesitating at a crossroads.
Some seem to wait, others withdraw
Into the glittering that flows without light.

Man's voyage, and woman's, is long, longer
    than life,
It is a star at the end of the road, a sky
That was shining, we thought, between two trees.
When the bucket touches the water that lifts it up,
There is joy, then the chain overwhelms it.

Le Puits, Les Ronces

Mais nous aimons ces puits qui veillent loin des routes
Car nous nous demandons qui vient vers eux
Dans les herbes barrées de ronces, attirés
Par ces sortes de dômes que font leurs lauzes
Au-dessus des buissons, là où commence
Le pays qui ne sait que l'éternel;
Qui s'arrête auprès d'eux aujourd'hui encore,
Qui les ouvre et se penche, en un autre monde.
Le fer rouillé résiste, il fait grand bruit
Puis grand silence quand retombe sur la pierre
La tôle qui sépare les deux ciels.

Et ce n'est qu'un instant de l'été, le grillon
Effrayé a repris, hors de la mort,
Son chant qui est matière faite voix
Et, peut-être, lumière mais pour rien.
Il a perçu que ces froissements d'herbes,
Ces mots, cette espérance, ne furent pas
Plus qu'il n'est, lui (si c'est le mot), parmi les ronces
Qui griffent nos visages mais ne sont
Que le rien qui griffe le rien dans la lumière.

The Well, the Brambles

But we love those wells that keep their vigil far from roads,
For we wonder who comes toward them
Through the grasses obstructed by brambles, drawn
By their stony domes rising
Above the bushes, where the country
That only knows eternity begins;
We wonder who pauses at them today,
Who opens them, and bends down over another world.
The rusted iron resists, there is a noise
Then a silence as deep, when the lid
That divides the two heavens falls back upon the stone.

And this is just a moment of summer, the startled
Cricket has taken up once more, outside death,
His song that is matter becoming voice
Or light, even, but perhaps for nothing.
He has perceived that these trampled grasses,
These words, these expectations, were not
More than he is himself (if this is the word) among the brambles
That scratch our faces but are only
Nothingness scratching nothingness in the summer's light.

La Rapidité des nuages

Le lit, la vitre auprès, la vallée, le ciel,
La magnifique rapidité de ces nuages.
La griffe de la pluie sur la vitre, soudain,
Comme si le néant paraphait le monde.

Dans mon rêve d'hier
Le grain d'autres années brûlait par flammes courtes
Sur le sol carrelé, mais sans chaleur.
Nos pieds nus l'écartaient comme une eau limpide.

Ô mon amie,
Comme était faible la distance entre nos corps!
La lame de l'épée du temps qui rôde
Y eût cherché en vain le lieu pour vaincre.

The Swiftness of the Clouds

The bed, the window next to it, the valley, the sky,
The glorious swiftness of the clouds.
The sudden scratching of the rain at the window,
As though nothingness were signing the world.

In my dream, yesterday,
The grain of years past was burning in brief flames
On the tiles of the floor, but without heat.
Our bare feet divided its clear water.

O my beloved,
How slight the distance between our bodies then!
The blade of time's wandering sword
Would have sought out in vain a place to triumph.

La Foudre

Il a plu, cette nuit.
Le chemin a l'odeur de l'herbe mouillée,
Puis, à nouveau, la main de la chaleur
Sur notre épaule, comme
Pour dire que le temps ne va rien nous prendre.

Mais là
Où le champ vient buter contre l'amandier,
Vois, un fauve a bondi
D'hier à aujourd'hui à travers les feuilles.

Et nous nous arrêtons, c'est hors du monde,

Et je viens près de toi,
J'achève de t'arracher du tronc noirci,
Branche, été foudroyé
De quoi la sève d'hier, divine encore, coule.

The Lightning

It rained, during the night.
The path smells of wet grass,
Then, once again, the hand of the heat
On our shoulder, to say
That time will never take anything from us.

But look,
There where the field runs up against the almond tree,
A beast of prey has sprung
From yesterday to today through the leaves.

And we stop, it is outside the world,

And I come toward you,
I finish tearing you from the blackened trunk,
Branch, lightning-struck summer
From which yesterday's sap flows, still divine.

L'Orée du bois

Tu me dis que tu aimes le mot ronce,
Et j'ai là l'occasion de te parler,
Sentant revivre en toi sans que tu le saches
Encore, cette ardeur qui fut toute ma vie.

Mais je ne puis rien te répondre : car les mots
Ont ceci de cruel qu'ils se refusent
À ceux qui les respectent et les aiment
Pour ce qu'ils pourraient être, non ce qu'ils sont.

Et ne me restent donc que des images,
Soit, presque, des énigmes, qui feraient
Que se détournerait, triste soudain,
Ton regard qui ne sait que l'évidence.

C'est comme quand il pleut le matin, vois-tu,
Et qu'on va soulever l'étoffe de l'eau
Pour se risquer plus loin que la couleur
Dans l'inconnu des flaques et des ombres.

The Edge of the Woods

You tell me you love the word *brambles,*
And this gives me a chance to talk to you,
Sensing the ardour that was my whole life
Well up again in you, even if you don't know it.

But there is no answer I can give, for words
Can be cruel: they will resist
Those who respect and love them
For what they could be and not for what they are.

And so all I have left are images,
Nothing but enigma, that is, and what
Would make you look away, suddenly sad,
Your eyes seeing only into what is.

Listen, it is the same with the morning rain
When you lift up the curtains of water
To venture out, and further than color,
Into the unknown of puddles and shadows.

II

Et pourtant, c'est bien l'aube, dans ce pays
Qui m'a bouleversé et que tu aimes.
La maison de ces quelques jours est endormie,
Nous nous sommes glissés dans l'éternel.

Et l'eau cachée dans l'herbe est encore noire,
Mais la rosée recommence le ciel.
L'orage de la nuit s'apaise, la nuée
A mis sa main de feu dans la main de cendre.

II

And yet, it really is dawn, in this country
That has stirred me so much and that you love.
The house of these last few days is sleeping,
And we have slipped into the eternal.

The water hidden in the grass is still in darkness,
But the dew has begun the sky once more.
The night storm has quieted, and the cloud
Has placed its fiery hand in the hand of ashes.

Une pierre

Viens, que je te dise à voix basse
Un enfant dont je me souviens,
Immobile comme il resta
À distance des autres vies.

Il n'a pas rejoint au matin
Ceux qui jouaient dans les arbres
À multiplier l'univers,
Ni couru à travers la plage
Vers plus de lumière encore.
Vois, pourtant, il a continué
Son chemin au pied de la dune,
Des traces de pas en sont preuves
Entre les chardons et la mer.

Et près d'eux tu peux voir s'emplir
De l'eau qui double le ciel
L'empreinte des pas plus larges
D'une compagne inconnue.

A Stone

Come, let me whisper to you of
A child I knew,
Separate as he was
From the others, motionless.

Mornings, he never joined
Those at play in the trees,
Adding worlds to worlds,
Nor would he run across the beach
Toward still more light.
Look, though, he has
Made his way at the base
Of the dunes—proof of it
Are these footprints between
The thistles and the sea.

And near them, you can see
That the water that reflects the sky
Is filling the larger footprints
Of an unknown woman going by.

Le Mot Ronce, *dis-tu*

Le mot ronce, dis-tu? Je me souviens
De ces barques échouées dans le varech
Que traînent les enfants les matins d'été
Avec des cris de joie dans les flaques noires

Car il en est, vois-tu, où demeure la trace
D'un feu qui y brûla à l'avant du monde
—Et sur le bois noirci, où le temps dépose
Le sel qui semble un signe mais s'efface,
Tu aimeras toi aussi l'eau qui brille.

Du feu qui va en mer la flamme est brève,
Mais quand elle s'éteint contre la vague,
Il y a des irisations dans la fumée.
Le mot ronce est semblable à ce bois qui sombre.

Et poésie, si ce mot est dicible,
N'est-ce pas de savoir, là où l'étoile
Parut conduire mais pour rien sinon la mort,

Aimer cette lumière encore? Aimer ouvrir
L'amande de l'absence dans la parole?

The Word *Brambles,* You Say

The word *brambles,* you say? Then I think of
Those boats stranded in sea-weed
That children drag on summer mornings
With cries of joy through dark pools of water.

Because in some, you see, there are traces
Of a fire that burned there at the prow of the world.
—And on the blackened wood where time has left
The salt that seems a sign but vanishes,
You too shall love the shimmering water.

Brief is the flame that goes out to sea,
But when it is quenched against the wave,
The smoke is filled with iridescence.
—The word *brambles* is like this sinking wood.

And poetry, if we can use this word,
Is it not still, there where the star
Seemed to beckon, but only toward death,

Knowing how to love this light? To love
To open the kernel of absence in words?

La Branche

Branche que je ramasse à l'orée des bois
Mais pour t'abandonner à la fin du monde,
Cachée parmi des pierres, dans l'abri
Où commence invisible l'autre chemin

(Car tout instant terrestre est un carrefour
Où, quand l'été s'achève, va notre ombre
Vers son autre pays dans les mêmes arbres,
Et rarement est-on venu reprendre
Une autre année la branche dont on courbe
Tout un été, distraitement, les herbes),

Branche, je pense à toi maintenant qu'il neige,
Je te vois resserrée sur le non-sens
Des quelques nœuds du bois, là où l'écorce
S'écaille, au gonflement de tes forces sombres,

Et je reviens, une ombre sur le sol blanc,
Vers ton sommeil qui hante ma mémoire,
Je te prends à ton rêve qui s'éparpille,
N'étant que d'eau pénétrée de lumière.
Puis je vais là où je sais que la terre
Se dérobe d'un coup, parmi les arbres,
Et je te jette aussi loin que je peux,
Je t'écoute qui rebondit de pierre en pierre.

(Non, je te veux
Tout un moment encore. Je vais, je prends
Le troisième chemin, que je voyais
Se perdre dans les herbes, sans que je sache
Pourquoi je n'entrais pas dans ses fourrés
Certes sombres, certes sans voix d'oiseaux dans les feuillages.
Je vais, je suis bientôt dans une maison

The Branch

Branch that I pick up at the edge of the woods,
But only to abandon you at the end of the world,
Beneath a pile of stones, in the shelter
Where, invisible, the other path begins

(For every earthly moment is a crossroads
Where, when summer ends, our shadow goes
Toward its other land in the same trees,
And rarely does one take up a second time
The branch with which all summer long
One bent the grasses absentmindedly),

Branch, I think of you now that it is snowing.
I see you drawn up into the meaninglessness
Of the few knots of wood, there where the bark
Is peeling, and your somber forces swell.

Then, a shadow on the white ground, I come back
Toward your slumber that haunts my memory,
I take you from your dreaming that suddenly scatters,
Being only water filled with light.
I go toward the place where I know
That the earth falls away all at once in the trees,
And I throw you as far as I can,
I listen to you bounding from stone to stone.

(No, I want you
For a moment more. And so I go on,
I take the third path, the one I used to see
Disappearing in the grasses, without knowing
Why I did not go into its dark
Thickets, where no birdsongs filled the trees.
I go on, and soon I am in a house

Où j'ai vécu jadis mais dont la voie
S'était perdue comme, quand la vie passe,
Des mots sont dits, sans qu'on s'en aperçoive,
Pour la dernière fois dans l'éternel.
Un feu brûle, dans une de ses salles toujours désertes,
Je l'écoute qui cherche dans le miroir
Des braises le rameau de la lumière,
Ainsi le dieu qui croit qu'il va créer
L'esprit, la vie, dans la nuit dont les nœuds
Sont serrés, infinis, labyrinthiques.

Puis je te pose, doucement, sur le lit des flammes,
Je te vois qui t'embrase dans ton sommeil,
Je suis penché, je tiens longtemps encore
Ta main, qui est l'enfance qui s'achève.)

Where once I used to live but whose way
Was lost, just as, when life passes,
Words are sometimes said for the last time
In the eternal, without our realizing it.
A fire is burning in one of the still empty rooms;
I listen to it as it seeks in the mirror
Of the embers the lost bough of light,
Like the god who believes he will create
Life and mind out of the night, whose knots
Are serried, are endless, are a labyrinth.

Then I place you gently on the bed of flames,
I watch you catch fire in your sleep,
I am bent over you, I keep your hand in mine
For a long time: it is childhood, dying.)

Sur des branches chargées de neige

I

D'une branche neigeuse à l'autre, de ces années
Qui ont passé sans qu'aucun vent n'effraie leurs feuilles,
Se font des éparpillements de la lumière
À des moments, comme nous avançons dans ce silence.

Et cette poudre ne retombe qu'infinie,
Nous ne savons plus bien si un monde existe
Encore, ou si nous recueillons sur nos mains mouillées
Un cristal de réalité parfaitement pure.

Couleurs avec le froid plus denses, bleus et pourpres
Qui appelez de plus loin que le fruit,
Êtes-vous notre rêve qui moins s'efface
Qu'il ne se fait la prescience et la voie?

Le ciel a bien lui-même ces nuées
Dont l'évidence est fille de la neige,
Et si nous nous tournons vers la route blanche,
C'est la même lumière et la même paix.

On Branches Heavy with Snow

From one snowy branch to the other, in these years
That have passed without a wind
Ever frightening their leaves,
Fragments of light scatter
At certain moments, as we go into the silence.

And this powder is boundless when it falls,
We cannot tell if a world still
Exists, or if our wet hands have grasped
Some crystal of reality, perfectly pure.

Colors that grow deeper with the cold, blues and purples
That call from further off than the fruit,
Are you our dream that does not so much vanish
As become prescience and path?

And yes, the sky itself has those clouds
Whose obviousness is the daughter of the snow,
And if we turn toward the whitened road,
It is the same light there, and the same peace.

II

Sauf, c'est vrai, que le monde n'a d'images
Que semblables aux fleurs qui trouent la neige
En mars, puis se répandent, toutes parées,
Dans notre rêverie d'un jour de fête,

Et qu'on se penche là, pour emporter
Des brassées de leur joie dans notre vie,
Bientôt les voici mortes, non tant dans l'ombre
De leur couleur fanée que dans nos cœurs.

Ardue est la beauté, presque une énigme,
Et toujours à recommencer l'apprentissage
De son vrai sens au flanc du pré en fleurs
Que couvrent par endroits des plaques de neige.

II

Except, of course, that in this world, images
Are like the flowers that pierce the snow
In March, then burst open in full splendor
In the dreams we have of festive days,

And should one bend over them, hoping to carry off
By the armful the joy that they promise,
See how soon they die, not so much in the shadow
Of their fading color as in our hearts.

Beauty is arduous, almost an enigma,
And endless is the task of learning its meaning
On the slopes of the flowering meadow,
Still covered here and there with plates of snow.

La Neige

Elle est venue de plus loin que les routes,
Elle a touché le pré, l'ocre des fleurs,
De cette main qui écrit en fumée,
Elle a vaincu le temps par le silence.

Davantage de lumière ce soir
À cause de la neige.
On dirait que des feuilles brûlent, devant la porte,
Et il y a de l'eau dans le bois qu'on rentre.

The Snow

It has come from further than the roads,
It has touched the meadow, the ochre of the flowers,
With that hand that writes in smoke,
It has vanquished time through silence.

More light this evening
Because of the snow.
You would think the leaves in front of the door were burning,
And there is water in the wood we bring in.

III

Par où la terre finit

I

Puisque c'est à la tombée de la nuit que prend son vol l'oiseau de Minerve, c'est le moment de parler de vous, chemins qui vous effacez de cette terre victime.

Vous avez été l'évidence, vous n'êtes plus que l'énigme. Vous inscriviez le temps dans l'éternité, vous n'êtes que du passé maintenant, par où la terre finit, là, devant nous, comme un bord abrupt de falaise.

Out by Where the Earth Ends

Since it is at nightfall that Minerva's owl takes flight, the moment has come to speak of you, paths that disappear from this victim earth.

Once there was no doubt about you, now you are nothing but enigma. Once you inscribed time in eternity, now you are only the past, out by where the earth ends, there, before us, like a sheer drop of cliff.

II

Une ombre de feuille ou de fleur se projetait sur une pierre, on s'asseyait à côté, on se retrouvait peintre chinois avec un peu de couleur à mêler à de l'encre noire.

C'était l'infini qui se faisait le fini, comme dans le territoire des bêtes. Ce qui partait savait revenir. Heureux le temps où, quand un chemin se perdait, on savait que c'était parce qu'il n'y avait pas de raison d'aller plus avant, de ce côté-ci de la fin du monde.

II

The shadow of a leaf or flower was cast upon a stone, we used to sit down beside it and feel like a Chinese painter with a bit of color to mix with black ink.

It was the infinite becoming the finite, as in the territories roamed by animals. What left knew how to return. How happy the time when, if a path disappeared, we knew it was only because there was no reason to go onward, on this side of the end of the world!

Tel qui allait du même pas que le ruisseau proche et se mêlait à lui en des points on ne savait guère si gués ou flaques, dans la lumière brisée des moucherons et des libellules.

Tel qui avait gravi une pente parmi les pins et les petits chênes puis débouchait à découvert devant tout un chaos de tertres boisés, certains barrés jusqu'à l'horizon de lignes de pierre nue.

Et cet autre, là-bas,—on rêvait que c'était un lac qu'on finirait par atteindre, il y aurait dans les herbes, abandonnée, faisant eau, une barque peinte de bleu.

III

The one that ran along with the nearby brook and at certain points blended with it, and one could hardly tell if these were fords or simple pools, in the light broken by the gnats and dragonflies.

The one that had climbed a slope among the pines and the little oaks, then opened onto a whole chaos of wooded knolls, some barred with lines of naked stone all the way to the horizon.

And that other one down there—we dreamed that it would eventually lead us to a lake, and in the grasses, abandoned and half full of water, there would be a boat, painted blue.

IV

Tel qui se faufilait comme une couleuvre sous les feuilles d'une autre année.

Il y a une minute, il n'était pas. Dans un instant, il ne serait plus.

IV

The one that wove like a snake beneath the leaves of another year.

A minute ago, it wasn't there. In another moment, it would no longer be.

V

Tel accourait, nous suivait. On se prenait à vouloir lui donner un nom.

Il s'était pris d'amitié pour la petite fille. Pour les huit ans de cette année-là; et jappait sans fin autour d'elle, à grands bonds et rebonds d'herbe mouillée.

Dormant parfois tout un jour, le nez dans un repli d'ombre.

V

The one that ran up to us and followed us along, we began to want to give it a name.

It had taken a liking to the little girl. To the eight years she had at the time; it yelped around her endlessly, jumping up again and again in leaps of wet grass.

Sleeping sometimes all day long, its nose in a patch of shadow.

Bouddhistes sans le savoir.

Et surtout pas « une voie ». Ils laissaient cela à notre gnose.

Essayant même de retenir, ironiquement, le pèlerin.

Belle image d'eux ces petits dieux du Japon qu'on voit auprès des villages, statues frustes de pierre grise qui ont une étoffe attachée au cou devant les quelques offrandes comme s'ils étaient des enfants qui vont manger leur œuf à la coque. Leur lieu de culte, chez nous: ces oratoires dont la grille rouillée ne ferme plus, où l'on perçoit au passage, demi-séchée, l'adoration odorante de fleurs mêlées à des feuilles.

VI

Buddhists without knowing it.

And above all, not a "way." They left that to our gnosis.

Trying even, mischievously, to hold the pilgrim back.

A perfect image of them would be those little gods you see near villages in Japan; worn gray stone statues, standing before a few humble offerings with a bit of cloth around the neck like children about to eat a soft-boiled egg. Their place of worship here, at home: those oratories whose rusted gates no longer shut and where you sense, as you pass by, the fragrant, half-withered adoration of flowers mixed with leaves.

VII

Passant par exemple devant les vieux cimetières dont les portes sont gardées closes par un nœud informe de fil de fer; et proposant de le dénouer, patiemment, d'entrer; de déchiffrer quelques noms, sur les pierres couvertes d'herbe; de repartir sans inquiétude ni hâte.

Puis de continuer jusque sur la hauteur où fut autrefois le village, que rappellent dans le rocher quelques éboulis dans les ronces; et d'avancer, avec précaution, vers le point d'où l'on domine les deux vallées, dont les lumières sont différentes. « Remarque, dit le génie des chemins, cette ferme là-bas dont il ne reste plus que les murailles sans toit, retenant des ombres très noires. Remarque, pour oublier. »

VII

Leading us, for example, to old cemeteries whose doors are kept closed by a shapeless knot of wire; proposing to undo it, patiently, and to go in; and make out a few names on the grass-covered stones; then leave without haste or concern.

Then to keep on going up to where the village once stood, its stony remains scattered in the brambles; and to proceed cautiously, toward the point that overlooks the two valleys, whose lights are different. "Notice that farm down there," whispers the angel of the paths, "only its walls are standing now, without a roof, and host to the darkest shadows. Notice, to forget."

VIII

Et où allait cet autre encore, c'était sans joie, sans beauté, on pataugeait, on se perdait dans la brume, mais pour finir, de deux souches de ciel rapprochées dans l'âtre de la montée qui s'achève jaillissait un rayon, le soleil du soir.

(Mais il n'est pas de chemins pour descendre chez les morts, malgré ce que dit Racine. En fait d'âmes, voici la graine qui vole, le fil de la Vierge, le moucheron. L'entrée au pays des morts se fait comme il est dit dans la légende celtique, par une route droite, bordée de ces auberges qui sont ouvertes toute la nuit. Route comme ce qu'il faut bien emprunter, soudain plus large et rapide, chaque fois qu'on approche d'une frontière.)

VIII

And where that other ended, it was without joy, or beauty, we floundered, we were lost in the mist, but at last there were these two stumps of sky suddenly closer in the hearth of our last steps, and from them a ray of light burst forth—, the evening sun.

(But there is no path that goes down to the dead, in spite of what Racine says. The souls, here, are seeds in flight, gossamer, gnats. The true way to the land of the dead, as the Celtic legend says, would be by a straight road, lined with those inns that stay open all night long. The kind of road, wider suddenly and quicker, you have to take each time you near a border.)

IX

Un qui tenait une coupe, où brillait le vin du ciel calme.

Un qui allait, eût-on dit, beyond the river and into the trees. *Un qui était notre voie lactée.*

Et il y en avait un encore plus large, et qui aimait accueillir nos ombres sur son sable, qui était lisse. Elles couraient loin en avant de nous car c'était le soir, et nous les sentions agitées, inquiètes. Mais l'ombre d'un oiseau les touchait parfois et les accompagnait un instant, avant de s'en écarter d'un brusque coup de sa rame.

IX

One that held a cup in which the wine of the peaceful sky shone.

One that seemed to go "beyond the river and into the trees." One that was our milky way.

And there was an even wider one that liked to welcome our shadows on its smooth sands. They ran far ahead of us, for it was evening, and we sensed them agitated, uneasy. But the shadow of a bird would sometimes touch them and go along with them for a moment, before breaking off with a sudden thrust of its oars.

Chemins,
Non, ce n'est pas dans vos rumeurs que rien s'achève.
Vous êtes un enfant qui joue de la flûte
Et dont les doigts confiants recréent le monde
De rien qu'un peu de terre où se prend le souffle.

Et le temps a posé
Sa main sur son épaule, et se laisse aveugle
Conduire sous la voûte des nombres purs.

X

Paths,
No, nothing comes to an end in your rustling.
You are a child playing the flute
And whose trusting fingers recreate the world
From nothing but a bit of earth and breath.

And time has placed
Its hand upon his shoulder, and lets itself
Be blindly led beneath the vault of numbers.

Là où creuse le vent

I

On dit qu'un dieu chercha
Sur les eaux closes
Comme un rapace veut
Sa proie lointaine

Et d'un cri répété,
Rauque, désert,
Créa le temps qui brille
Où la vague se creuse.

La nuit couvre le jour
Puis se retire,
Son écume déferle
Sur les pierres d'ici.

Qu'est-ce que Dieu, s'il n'a
Que le temps pour œuvre,
A-t-il voulu mourir
Faute de pouvoir naître?

En vain fut son combat
Contre l'absence.
Il jeta le filet,
Elle tint le glaive.

II

Mais demeure l'éclair
Au-dessus du monde
Comme à un gué, cherchant
De pierre en pierre.

There in the Hollows of the Wind

I

They say a god searched
Over sealed waters
Like a rapacious bird
Its distant prey

And with a raucous,
Solitary cry
Created Time that shines
In the hollows of the wave.

Night covers day
Then withdraws,
Its foam unfurls
Upon the stones close by.

What is God, if his
Only work is time,
Has he wanted to die
Not knowing birth?

In vain his battle
Against absence.
He threw out his net,
Absence held the sword.

II

But the lightning remains
Poised above the world
As though fording a stream
From stone to stone.

Est-ce que la beauté
N'a été qu'un rêve,
Le visage aux yeux clos
De la lumière?

Non, puisqu'elle a reflet
En nous, et c'est la flamme
Qui dans l'eau du bois mort
Se baigne nue.

C'est le corps exalté
Par un miroir
Comme un feu prend, soudain,
Dans un cercle de pierres.

Et a sens le mot joie
Malgré la mort
Là où creuse le vent
Ces braises claires.

III

Suffisance des jours
Qui vont vers l'aube
Par éblouissements
Dans le ciel nocturne.

Le glaive, le filet
Ne sont plus qu'une
Main, qui étreint en paix
La nuque brève.

L'âme est, illuminée,
Comme un nageur
Qui se jette, d'un coup,
Sous la lumière

Has beauty been
Only a dream,
The face of the light
But with eyes closed?

No, since its reflection
Is in us: the flame
That bathes naked
In the dead wood's water.

It is the body exalted
By a mirror
As a fire catches, suddenly,
In a circle of stones.

And the word joy has meaning
In spite of death
There where the wind will stir
These burning embers.

III
Sufficient the days
That go towards dawn
In bursts of light
In the night sky.

The sword, the net now
Make only a single
Hand, that clasps in peace
The fragile neck.

Illuminated, the soul is
Like a swimmer
Who plunges, all at once,
Beneath the light

Et ses yeux sont fermés,
Son corps est nu,
Sa bouche veut le sel,
Non le langage.

And his eyes are closed,
His body naked,
His mouth wants salt,
Not language.

Dedham, vu de Langham

Dedham, vu de Langham. L'été est sombre
Où des nuages se rassemblent. On pourrait croire
Que tout cela, haies, villages au loin,
Rivière, va finir. Que la terre n'est pas
Même l'éternité des bêtes, des arbres,
Et que ce son de cloches, qui a quitté
La tour de cette église, se dissipe,
Bruit simplement parmi les bruits terrestres,
Comme l'espoir que l'on a quelquefois
D'avoir perçu des signes sur des pierres
Tombe, dès qu'on voit mieux ces traits en désordre,
Ces taches, ces sursauts de la chose nue.

Mais tu as su mêler à ta couleur
Une sorte de sable qui du ciel
Accueille l'étincellement dans la matière.
Là où c'était le hasard qui parlait
Dans les éboulements, dans les nuées,
Tu as vaincu, d'un début de musique,
La forme qui se clôt dans toute vie.
Tu écoutes le bruit d'abeilles des choses claires,
Son gonflement parfois, cet absolu
Qui vibre dans le pré parmi les ombres,
Et tu le laisses vivre en toi, et tu t'allèges
De n'être plus ainsi hâte ni peur.

Ô peintre,
Comme une main presse une grappe, main divine,
De toi dépend le vin; de toi, que la lumière
Ne soit pas cette griffe qui déchire
Toute forme, toute espérance, mais une joie

Dedham, Seen from Langham

Dedham, seen from Langham. The summer is somber,
Clouds are gathering. You might think that
The whole scene, the hedges, the distant villages,
The river, was about to vanish. That the earth
Was not even the eternity of the flocks and trees,
And that the chiming of bells, flung from
The church steeple, was also drifting away,
One more sound among the sounds of earth,
As the hope one sometimes has
Of having discovered signs written on stones
Falls when one examines more closely the tangle
Of markings: those shudders on the face of earth.

But you knew how to mix with your color
A kind of sand which welcomes
The glitterings of the sky in matter.
Where it was chance that spoke
Among the rubble, in the clouds,
You vanquished
With the beginnings of a music
The form which is the dead face of all life.
You listen to the sound of bees in things filled with light,
To the way the buzzing sometimes seems to swell
Into that absolute in the meadow's shadows,
And you let it live in you, more transparent,
Since now you know neither haste nor fear.

O painter,
The wine is your gift
Your hand, your divine hand,
As if pressing the grape; and thanks to you
The light is no longer that claw

Dans les coupes même noircies du jour de fête.
Peintre de paysage, grâce à toi
Le ciel s'est arrêté au-dessus du monde
Comme l'ange au-dessus d'Agar quand elle allait,
Le cœur vide, dans le dédale de la pierre.

Et que de plénitude est dans le bruit,
Quand tu le veux, du ruisseau qui dans l'herbe
A recueilli le murmure des cloches,
Et que d'éternité se donne dans l'odeur
De la fleur la plus simple! C'est comme si
La terre voulait bien ce que l'esprit rêve.

Et la petite fille qui vient en rêve
Jouer dans la prairie de Langham, et regarde
Quelquefois ce Dedham au loin, et se demande
Si ce n'est pas là-bas qu'il faudrait vivre,
Cueille pour rien la fleur qu'elle respire
Puis la jette et l'oublie; mais ne se rident
Dans l'éternel été
Les eaux de cette vie ni de cette mort.

II

Peintre,
Dès que je t'ai connu je t'ai fait confiance,
Car tu as beau rêver tes yeux sont ouverts
Et risques-tu ta pensée dans l'image
Comme on trempe la main dans l'eau, tu prends le fruit
De la couleur, de la forme brisées,
Tu le poses réel parmi les choses dites.

Peintre,
J'honore tes journées, qui ne sont rien
Que la tâche terrestre, délivrée

That tears apart every form, every hope,
But rather joy, flowing in festive cups, however dark.
Thanks to you, landscape painter,
The sky has paused above the world
As did the angel above Hagar when she went,
With empty heart, into the labyrinths of stone.

And when you wish it so, how much fullness
Dwells within the murmur of the brook in the grass
As it gathers up the distant sounds of the church bells,
And how much eternity is offered in the scent
Of the simplest flower! It is as though earth
Consented gladly to what the spirit dreams of.

And the little girl who comes in dream
To play in the fields of Langham, and who
Sometimes looks toward Dedham in the distance, wondering
If it is not over there that one should live,
Picks, aimlessly, the flower she is smelling,
Then throws it aside and thinks no more
About it—but the waters of life,
Or death, are not rippled at all,
In the eternal summer.

II

Painter,
As soon as I knew you, I trusted you,
For even when you are dreaming, your eyes are open,
And should you risk your vision in images,
As one might plunge a hand into water, you always seize
The fruit of broken form, of broken color,
And you place it, real, among the names of things.

Painter,
I give praise to your days, which are nothing more
Than the earthly task, delivered

Des hâtes qui l'aveuglent. Rien que la route
Mais plus lente là-bas dans la poussière.
Rien que la cime
Des montagnes d'ici mais dégagée,
Un instant, de l'espace. Rien que le bleu
De l'eau prise du puits dans le vert de l'herbe
Mais pour la conjonction, la métamorphose
Et que monte la plante d'un autre monde,
Palmes, grappes de fruits serrées encore,
Dans l'accord de deux tons, notre unique vie.
Tu peins, il est cinq heures dans l'éternel
De la journée d'été. Et une flamme
Qui brûlait par le monde se détache
Des choses et des rêves, transmutée.
On dirait qu'il ne reste qu'une buée
Sur la paroi de verre.

Peintre,
L'étoile de tes tableaux est celle en plus
De l'infini qui peuple en vain les mondes.
Elle guide les choses vers leur vraie place,
Elle enveloppe là leur dos de lumière,
Plus tard,
Quand la main du dehors déchire l'image,
Tache de sang l'image,
Elle sait rassembler leur troupe craintive
Pour le piétinement de nuit, sur un sol nu.

Et quelquefois,
Dans le miroir brouillé de la dernière heure,
Elle sait dégager, dit-on, comme une main
Essuie la vitre où a brillé la pluie,
Quelques figures simples, quelques signes
Qui brillent au-delà des mots, indéchiffrables
Dans l'immobilité du souvenir.
Formes redessinées, recolorées

From the haste that blinds it. Nothing more
Than the road, the slower road, up there
In the dust. Nothing more
Than the mountaintops of our world, but freed
For a moment from space. Nothing but the blue
Of the water drawn from the well in the green of the grass,
But for conjunction and metamorphosis,
And so that the plant of another world may spring up,
Palms, clusters of fruit still pressed close together,
In the resolution of the two colors, our sole life.
You paint, it is five o'clock in the eternity
Of the summer day. And a flame
That burned throughout the world breaks free
From things, from dreams, transmuted.
It seems that nothing remains but a faint cloud
Of mist on the surface of the alembic.

Painter,
The star in your landscapes is the one missing
In the infinite that crowds in vain the worlds.
It guides things toward their true places,
Then throws a cloak of light around their shoulders,
And later,
When the hand from the outside tears apart the image,
And splatters it with blood,
The star brings their frightened flocks together again
For the hoofbeats at night, against the naked earth.

And sometimes,
In the blurred mirror of the last hour,
They say that the star knows how to draw forth,
As a hand wipes a window pane that shone with rain,
A few simple figures, a few signs
Gleaming beyond words, indecipherable
In the motionlessness of memory,
Forms that are drawn and colored anew

A l'horizon qui ferme le langage,
C'est comme si la foudre qui frappait
Suspendait, dans le même instant, presque éternel,
Son geste d'épée nue, et comme surprise
Redécouvrait le pays de l'enfance,
Parcourant ses chemins; et, pensive, touchait
Les objets oubliés, les vêtements
Dans de vieilles armoires, les deux ou trois
Jouets mystérieux de sa première
Allégresse divine. Elle, la mort,
Elle défait le temps qui va le monde,
Montre le mur qu'éclaire le couchant,
Et mène autour de la maison vers la tonnelle
Pour offrir, ô bonheur ici, dans l'heure brève,
Les fruits, les voix, les reflets, les rumeurs,
Le vin léger dans rien que la lumière.

On the horizon that closes our language;
It is as though the lightning, as it struck,
Held back its naked sword, and with surprise,
At this very instant, almost eternal,
Rediscovered the land of childhood,
Wandered along its paths; and touched once more,
With pensive hands, things long forgotten; the clothes
That languish in old closets, the two or three
Mysterious toys from the child's first moments
Of joyfulness divine. This light, this death
Undoes time as it roams throughout the world;
Shows us the wall all lit up at sunset
And leads us around the house and toward the arbor
To offer, for one brief moment, O blissfulness,
The fruit, the voices, the shadows, the sounds,
The gentle wine, in nothing but the light.

IV

Psyché devant le château d'Amour

Il rêva qu'il ouvrait les yeux, sur des soleils
Qui approchaient du port, silencieux
Encore, feux éteints; mais doublés dans l'eau grise
D'une ombre où foisonnait la future couleur.

Puis il se réveilla. Qu'est-ce que la lumière?
Qu'est-ce que peindre ici, de nuit? Intensifier
Le bleu d'ici, les ocres, tous les rouges,
N'est-ce pas de la mort plus encore qu'avant?

Il peignit donc le port mais le fit en ruine,
On entendait l'eau battre au flanc de la beauté
Et crier des enfants dans des chambres closes,
Les étoiles étincelaient parmi les pierres.

Mais son dernier tableau, rien qu'une ébauche,
Il semble que ce soit Psyché qui, revenue,
S'est écroulée en pleurs ou chantonne, dans l'herbe
Qui s'enchevêtre au seuil du château d'Amour.

Psyche before the Castle of Love

He dreamed that he was opening his eyes onto suns
As they drew near the harbor; silent,
Without light, but mirrored in the gray water
By the shadow of a color to be.

Then he awoke. What is light? And what does it mean
To paint here, in the night? To intensify
The blue we see, the ochres, all the reds,
Is this not death even more than before?

And so he painted the harbor, but in ruins,
You could hear the water lapping at beauty's flank
And children crying in closed rooms,
The stars sparkled among the stones.

But in his last painting, only a sketch,
It seems it is Psyche who has returned
And has collapsed in tears, or hums a tune,
In the tangled grasses of the castle of Love.

Le Haut du monde

Je sors,
Il y a des milliers de pierres dans le ciel,
J'entends
De toute part le bruit de la nuit en crue.
Est-il vrai, mes amis,
Qu'aucune étoile ne bouge?

Est-il vrai
Qu'aucune de ces barques pourtant chargées
D'on dirait plus que la simple matière
Et qui semblent tournées vers un même pôle
Ne frémisse soudain, ne se détache
De la masse des autres laissée obscure?

Est-il vrai
Qu'aucune de ces figures aux yeux clos
Qui sourient à la proue du monde dans la joie
Du corps qui vaque à rien que sa lumière
Ne s'éveille, n'écoute? N'entende au loin
Un cri qui soit d'amour, non de désir?

The Top of the World

I

I go out,
There are thousands of stones in the sky,
I can hear
All around me the surging sounds of night.
Is it true, my friends,
That not a single star is stirring?

Is it true
That not one of these barks loaded
You would think with more than simple matter
And that seem turned toward the same pole,
Shudders suddenly and breaks free
From the mass of the others, left behind, dark?

Is it true
That not one of these figures, with eyes closed,
That smile at the prow of the world in the joy
Of the body that attends to nothing but its light,
Awakens and listens, hearing in the distance
A cry filled with love, not with desire?

II

Elle ouvrirait, sans bruit,
Elle se risquerait dans le vent de mer
Telle une jeune fille qui sort de nuit
Soulevant une lampe qui répand
Sa clarté, qui l'effraye aussi, sur ses épaules,
Et se retourne, mais le monde va sans réponse,
Le bruit des pas de ceux qui devraient ouvrir
Leur porte sous les arbres, et la rejoindre
Ne sonne pas encore dans la vallée.

Les choses sont si confiantes pourtant,
L'agneau si complaisant à la main qui tue,

Et les regards sont si intenses parfois,
Les voix se troublent si mystérieusement quand on prononce
Certains mots pour demain, ou au secret
Des fièvres et des invites de la nuit.
Est-il vrai que les mots soient sans promesse,
Éclair immense en vain,

Coffre qui étincelle mais plein de cendres?

II

This one would rise up, soundlessly,
And venture forth in the sea wind,
Like a young girl who goes out at night
Holding high a lamp that pours out
Its light, which frightens her, upon her shoulders,
And who looks about her, though the world is silent;
The footsteps of those who should open
Their doors beneath the trees and join her
Cannot yet be heard in the valley.

And yet, things seem so trusting,
The lamb gives itself so willingly
To the hand that kills.

And the looks one exchanges are sometimes so intense,
The voices grow so mysteriously troubled when certain
Words are spoken for tomorrow, or in the secret depths
Of the feverish invitations of night.
Is it true that words carry no promise,
A vast and senseless flash of lightning,

A glittering chest, but full of ashes?

III

En d'autres temps, mes amis,
Nous aurions écouté, ne parlant plus
Soudain,
Bruire la pluie de nuit sur les tuiles sèches.

Nous aurions vu, courbé
Sous l'averse, courant
La tête protégée par le sac de toile,
Le berger rassembler ses bêtes. Nous aurions cru
Que le couteau de la foudre dévie
Parfois, compassionné,
Sur le dos laineux de la terre.

Nous aurions aperçu, qui se dispersent
Chaque fois que c'est l'aube,
Les rêves qui déposent, couronnés d'or,
Leur étincellement près d'une naissance.

III

There were times, my friends,
When, falling silent
All at once,
We would have listened to the sounds
Of the night rain on the dry tiles.

We would have seen the shepherd,
Bowed beneath the sudden downpour,
His head covered with a canvas sack,
Running to bring together his sheep.
We would have hoped that the knife
Of the lightning might sometimes,
In compassion,
Slip away from earth's fleecy back.

We would have caught a glimpse
Of the dreams that vanish with every dawn,
The gold-crowned dreams that set
Their glittering gifts besides the newborn child.

IV

Et fût-elle venue
S'asseoir auprès de nous, l'incohérente,
La vieille qui n'a plus que le souvenir,
Reste, l'un d'entre nous
Eût dit, reste, détends tes mains noircies par la fumée,
Parle-nous, instruis-nous, ô vagabonde.

Le ciel était scellé pourtant, comme aujourd'hui,
La barque de chaque chose, venue chargée
D'un blé du haut du monde, restait bâchée
À notre quai nocturne, brillant à peine
De simplement la pluie dans le vent de mer.

Et on rentrait le soir les mêmes bêtes lasses,
La mort était servante parmi nous
À recueillir le lait qui a goût de cendre.

IV

And had she come
To sit beside us, the old woman
Who makes no sense, who has only her memories,
One of us would have said, stay,
Relax those hands blackened by the smoke,
Talk to us, teach us things, O vagabond.

The heavens were sealed, however,
As they are today,
The boat of each thing that had come in
Loaded with a wheat from the heights of the world
Remained moored at our nocturnal pier,
Shimmering faintly from just the rain
Falling in the winds of the sea.

And at evening the same weary herds were brought in,
Death served among us,
Taking in the milk that has the taste of ashes.

V

Je sors.
Je rêve que je sors dans la nuit de neige.
Je rêve que j'emporte
Avec moi, loin, dehors, c'est sans retour,
Le miroir de la chambre d'en haut, celui des étés
D'autrefois, la barque à la proue de laquelle, simples,
Nous allions, nous interrogions, dans le sommeil
D'étés qui furent brefs comme est la vie.

En ce temps-là
C'est par le ciel qui brillait dans son eau
Que les mages de nos sommeils, se retirant,
Répandaient leurs trésors dans la chambre obscure.

V

I go out.
I dream that I am going out into the snowy night.
I dream that I am carrying
With me, far, outside, there is no turning back,
The mirror from the upstairs bedroom, the mirror from
Summers past, the boat at whose prow
We, simple, pushed forward, questioning,
Deep in the sleep of summers that were brief, as life is.

In those days
It was through the sky gleaming in the mirror's waters
That the magi of our sleep, as they withdrew,
Would spread out their treasures in the darkened room.

VI

Et la beauté du monde s'y penchait
Dans le bruissement du ciel nocturne,
Elle mirait son corps dans l'eau fermée
Des dormeurs, qui se ramifie entre des pierres.
Elle approchait bouche et souffle confiants
De leurs yeux sans lumière. Elle eût aimé
Qu'au repli de sa robe fermée encore
Paraisse sous l'épaule le sein plus clair,
Puis le jour se levait autour de toi,
Terre dans le miroir, et le soleil
Ourlait ta nuque nue d'une buée rouge.

Mais maintenant
Me voici hors de la maison dont rien ne bouge
Puisqu'elle n'est qu'un rêve. Je vais, je laisse
N'importe où, contre un mur, sous les étoiles,
Ce miroir, notre vie. Que la rosée
De la nuit se condense et coule, sur l'image.

VI

And in the rustling of the night sky
The beauty of the world bent down
To see her body reflected in the closed water
Of the sleepers, which branches out among the stones.
She brought trusting mouth and breath
Close to their lightless eyes. She would have wanted
Her brighter breast to appear beneath the shoulder
In the folds of her still closed robes,
Then day was rising around you,
Our earth in the mirror, and the sunlight
Hemmed your bare neck with a red band of mist.

But here I am now
Standing outside the house; everything is motionless
Since it is only a dream. And so I go on, leaving,
It hardly matters where, against a wall, beneath the stars,
This mirror, our life. And may night's dew
Condense and flow, over the images.

Ô galaxies
Poudroyantes au loin
De la robe rouge.

Rêves,
Troupeau plus noir, plus serré sur soi que les pierres.

Je vais,
Je passe près des amandiers sur la terrasse.
Le fruit est mûr.
J'ouvre l'amande et son cœur étincelle.

Je vais.
Il y a cet éclair immense devant moi,
Le ciel,
L'agneau sanglant dans la paille.

VII

O galaxies
Of the red dress
Glittering like the sands of a distant shore.

Dreams,
A flock, darker,
More tightly pressed together than stones.

I go on,
I pass by the almond trees on the terrace.
The fruit is ripe.
I open the almond and its heart sparkles.

I go on.
There is that immense flash of lightning
In front of me,
The sky,
The lamb bleeding in the straw.

Une pierre

Ils aimaient ce miroir
Dont le cadre écaillé s'ornait encore
Des cornes d'abondance de l'âge d'or.
Deux figures dansantes s'y faisaient face,
Ces épaules, ces ventres étaient nus,
Ces mains
Se touchaient, s'étreignaient,
Mais c'est vrai que les yeux ne se rencontraient pas.

Ils ont placé
Le miroir dans la terre, sous la neige,
Comme du grain; comme l'épi de ciel
Qui doit pourrir longtemps dans la boue du monde.

A Stone

They loved that mirror
Whose frame, though chipping away, was still
Adorned with horns of plenty from the golden age.
Two dancing figures faced each other,
The shoulders and bellies were bare,
The hands
Touched, clasped one another,
But the eyes, it is true, did not meet.

They put
The mirror in the ground, under the snow,
Like grain; like the corn of heaven
That must rot for a long time in the mud of the world.

V

L'Agitation du rêve

Dans ce rêve le fleuve encore: c'est l'amont,
Une eau serrée, violente, où des troncs d'arbres
S'entrechoquent, dévient; de toute part
Des rivages stériles m'environnent,
De grands oiseaux m'assaillent, avec un cri
De douleur et d'étonnement,—mais moi, j'avance
À la proue d'une barque, dans une aube.
J'y ai amoncelé des branches, me dit-on,
En tourbillons s'élève la fumée,
Puis le feu prend, d'un coup, deux colonnes torses,
Tout un porche de foudre. Je suis heureux
De ce ciel qui crépite, j'aime l'odeur
De la sève qui brûle dans la brume.

Et plus tard je remue des cendres, dans un âtre
De la maison où je viens chaque nuit,
Mais c'est déjà du blé, comme si l'âme
Des choses consumées, à leur dernier souffle,
Se détachait de l'épi de matière
Pour se faire le grain d'un nouvel espoir.
Je prends à pleines mains cette masse sombre
Mais ce sont des étoiles; je déplie
Les draps de ce silence, mais découvre
Très lointaine, très proche la forme nue
De deux êtres qui dorment, dans la lumière
Compassionnée de l'aube, qui hésite
À effleurer du doigt leurs paupières closes
Et fait que ce grenier, cette charpente,
Cette odeur du blé d'autrefois, qui se dissipe,
C'est encore leur lieu, et leur bonheur.

The Restlessness of the Dream

I

In this dream, the river again: upstream, now,
A narrow, violent water, filled with tree trunks
That collide and glance off one another; I am
Surrounded on all sides by lifeless shores,
Giant birds assail me with a cry
Full of anguish and amazement—but I go on
At the prow of a boat, in a dawn light.
I have made, I am told, a pile of branches,
The smoke rises in swirls,
Then all at once the fire catches, two wreathed columns,
A sudden porch of lightning. I am happy with
This crackling sky, I love the smell
Of the sap burning in the mist.

And later I am stirring ashes in a fireplace
In the house I come to, every night,
But already they are wheat, as though
The soul of things past, at the moment of
Their last breath, broke free from the husk of matter
To become the seed of a new hope.
I take up by the handful this somber heap,
But these are stars; I unfold
The sheets of this silence, but discover,
Very deep, very near, the naked form
Of two beings sleeping in the compassionate
Light of dawn, which hesitates to graze
Their closed eyelids with its finger
And ensures that this granary beneath its beams,
This smell of the wheat of years gone by
That slowly vanishes into the air,
That these remain a place for them, and happiness.

Je dois me délivrer de ces images.
Je m'éveille et me lève et marche. Et j'entre
Dans le jardin de quand j'avais dix ans,
Qui ne fut qu'une allée, bien courte, entre deux masses
De terre mal remuée, où les averses
Laissent longtemps des flaques où se prirent
Les premières lumières que j'aie aimées.
Mais c'est la nuit maintenant, je suis seul,
Les êtres que j'ai connus dans ces années
Parlent là-haut et rient, dans une salle
Dont tombe la lueur sur l'allée; et je sais
Que les mots que j'ai dits, décidant parfois
De ma vie, sont ce sol, cette terre noire.
Autour de moi le dédale, infini,
D'autres menus jardins avec leurs serres
Défaites, leurs tuyaux sur des plates-bandes
Derrière des barrières, leurs appentis
Où des meubles cassés, des portraits sans cadre,
Des brocs, et parfois des miroirs comme à l'aguet
Sous des bâches, prêts à s'ouvrir aux feux qui passent,
Furent aussi, hors du temps, ma première
Conscience de ce monde où l'on va seul.
Vais-je pouvoir reprendre à la glaise dure
Ces bouts de fer rouillés, ces éclats de verre,
Ces morceaux de charbon? Agenouillé,
Je détache de l'infini l'inexistence
Et j'en fais des figures, d'une main
Que je distingue mal, tant est la nuit
Précipitée, violente par les mondes.
Que lointaine est ici l'aube du signe!
J'ébauche une constellation mais tout se perd.

I must free myself from these images.
I awake, then get up and walk. I go into
The garden I knew as a child of ten,
Which was really just a short walkway
Between two patches of poorly toiled earth
Where the rainstorms left lingering puddles
That caught the first lights I loved.
But it is night now, I am alone,
The people I knew in those days
Are laughing and talking up there in a room
Whose feeble light gleams down on the walkway;
And I know that the words that I have spoken,
Sometimes determining the course of my life,
Are now this ground, this dark earth.
All around me the endless maze
Of other tiny gardens with their paltry
Greenhouses, their hoses lying on the flowerbeds
Behind fences, their sheds filled with
Broken furniture, pictures without frames,
Old pots, and sometimes mirrors that seem
Watchful beneath the pieces of tarpaulin,
Ready to give themselves to the passing fires;
These things, too, were my first awarenesses,
Outside time, of this world where we walk alone.
Will I be able to wrest from the hard clay
These pieces of rusted iron, these bits of glass,
These lumps of charcoal? Kneeling down,
I tear the inexistent from the infinite
And draw figures with it, my hand
Hardly visible, so rapid, violent,
Is the night that is drifting among the worlds.
How unlikely here the dawn of signs!
I sketch out a constellation, but everything fades away.

II

Et je lève les yeux, je l'ose enfin,
Et je vois devant moi, dans le ciel nu,
Passer la barque qui revint, parfois sans lumière,
Dans tant des rêves qui miroitent dans le sable
De la très longue rive de cette nuit.

Je regarde la barque, qui hésite.
Elle a tourné comme si des chemins
Se dessinaient pour elle sur la houle
Qui parcourt doucement, brisant l'écume,
L'immensité de l'ombre de l'étoile.

Et qui sont-ils, à bord? Un homme, une femme
Qui se détachent noirs de la fumée
D'un feu qu'ils entretiennent à la proue.
De l'homme, de la femme le désir
Est donc ce feu au dédale des mondes.

II

And I raise my eyes, at last I dare to,
And I see passing before me in the naked sky
The boat that reappeared, sometimes without light,
In so many of the dreams that shimmer in the sands
Of this night's long stretches of shore.

I look at the boat, as it hesitates.
It has turned, as though paths
Were traced for it across the rising surge
Of the waves that gently runs, breaking its foam,
Through the immensity of the star's shadow.

And who is that on board? A man, a woman
Who stand out darkly from the smoke
Of a fire they are tending at the prow.
And thus man's desire, and woman's,
Is this fire that burns in the maze of the worlds.

III

Je referme les yeux. Et m'apparaît
Maintenant, dans le flux de la mémoire,
Une coupe de terre rouge, dont des flammes
Débordent sur la main qui la soulève
Au-dessus de la barque qui s'éloigne.

Et c'est là un enfant, qui me demande
De m'approcher, mais il est dans un arbre,
Les reflets s'enchevêtrent dans les branches.
Qui es-tu? dis-je. Et lui à moi, riant :
Qui es-tu? Puisque tu ne sais pas souffler la flamme.

Qui es-tu? Vois, moi je souffle le monde,
Il fera nuit, je ne te verrai plus,
Veux-tu que ne nous reste que la lumière?
—Mais je ne sais répondre, de par un charme
Qui m'a étreint, de plus loin que l'enfance.

III

I close my eyes again. And there appears
Before me now, in the flow of memory,
The image of a cup made of red earth, whose
Flames overflow onto the hand that lifts it up
Above the boat as it vanishes.

And the cup is a child, and he asks me
To draw near, but he is in a tree,
There are tangles of light in the branches.
Who are you? I say. And he, laughingly: Who are you?
Since you do not know how to blow out the flame.

Who are you? Look, I blow out the world,
It will be night, I will no longer see you,
Do you want only light?
—But I cannot answer, for I am seized
By a spell from further off than childhood.

IV

Et je m'éloigne et vais vers le rivage.
La barque, et d'autres barques, y sont venues.
Mais tout y est silence, même l'eau claire.
Les figures de proue ont les yeux encore
Clos, à l'avant de ces lumières closes.

Et les rameurs sont endormis, le front
Dans leurs bras repliés en dehors des siècles.
La marque sur leur épaule, rouge sang,
Tristement brille encore, dans la brume
Que ne dissipe pas le vent de l'aube.

IV

I leave and move off toward the shore.
The boat, with other boats, has landed, now.
But everything is silent, even the limpid waters.
The eyes of the figureheads are still
Shut, at the prow of these closed lights.

And the oarsmen have gone to sleep, their foreheads
Resting on arms folded outside time.
The mark on their shoulders, red as blood is,
Still gleams sadly in the mist
That the winds of dawn cannot dispel.

Le Pays du sommet des arbres

I

L'enfant semblait errer au sommet de l'arbre,
On ne comprenait pas son corps, enveloppé
D'un feu, d'une fumée, que la lumière
Trouait d'un coup, parfois, comme une rame.

Il montait, descendait un peu, il s'arrêtait,
Il s'éloignait entre les pyramides
Du pays du sommet des arbres, qui sont rouges
Par leur flanc qui retient le soleil encore.

L'enfant allait chantant, rêvant sa vie.
Était-il seul en son jardin de palmes?
On dit que le soleil s'attarde parfois
Pour une nuit, au port d'un rêve simple.

On dit aussi que le soleil est une barque
Qui passe chaque soir la cime du ciel.
Les morts sont à l'avant, qui voient le monde
Se redoubler sans fin d'autres étoiles.

The Land of the Treetops

I

The child seemed to wander about at the top of the tree.
It was hard to make out the body, enveloped
In a fire, in a smoke, that the light would sometimes
Pierce, like an oar that is striking water.

He would climb up, then come down a little and stop.
He would rove among the pyramids
Of the land of the treetops whose flanks
Are still bathing in the sun's red light.

The child went along singing, dreaming his life.
Was he alone in his garden of palms?
They say that the sun sometimes lingers
For a night, in the harbor of a simple dream.

They also say that the sun is a bark
That crosses the summit of the sky each evening.
The dead are at the prow; they see the world
Endlessly duplicated by other stars.

II

L'enfant redescendit plus tard, de branche en branche
Dans ce qui nous parut un ciel étoilé.
Rien ne distinguait plus dans ce silence
La cime bleue des arbres et des mondes.

Il chantait, il riait, il était nu,
Son corps était d'avant que l'homme, la femme
Ne se fassent distincts pour retrouver
Criant, dans une joie, une espérance.

Il était le chant même. Qui s'interrompt
Parfois, le pied cherchant l'appui qui manque,
Puis qui reprend et, dirait-on, se parle, telles deux voix
À l'avant d'une barque qui s'éloigne.

On dit que la lumière est un enfant
Qui joue, qui ne veut rien, qui rêve ou chante.
Si elle vient à nous c'est par jeu encore,
Touchant le sol d'un pied distrait, qui serait l'aube.

II

Later, the child climbed down, passing from branch to branch
Through what seemed to us a starry sky.
Nothing made different, in the silence,
The blue summit of the trees and of the worlds.

He was singing and laughing, he was naked,
His body was from before the time
When man and woman made themselves distinct so as to find,
With the cry of pleasure, a new hope as well.

He was song itself. The song that breaks off,
Sometimes, its foot feeling for something firm,
Then starts again and seems to speak to itself,
Like two voices at the prow of a drifting boat.

It is said that light is a child
Who plays, who dreams or sings, wanting nothing.
If it comes toward us, it is still just to play,
Touching the ground with a heedless foot, that would be dawn.

La Nuit d'été

Tu as été sculptée à une proue,
Le temps t'a corrodée comme eût fait l'écume,
Il a fermé tes yeux une nuit d'orage,
Il a taché de sel ton sein presque nu.

Ô sainte aux mains brûlées que recolore
L'adoration d'encore quelques fleurs,
Sanctuaire de l'épars et du fugitif
Au bout des champs ensemencés de rouille,

Que de sommeil dans ta nuque penchée,
Que d'ombre, dans les feuilles sèches sur les dalles!
On dirait notre chambre d'une autre année,
Le même lit mais les persiennes closes.

The Summer Night

You were carved at a prow,
Time has worn you away, as the sea spray would have done.
It has closed your eyes on a stormy night,
Speckled with salt your nearly naked breast.

O holy young woman, whose hands, though charred, are colored
Again by the adoration of a few flowers,
Sanctuary, at the end of fields sown with rust,
For all that is scattered now, and transient,

How much sleep in the neck you bend,
How much shadow in the dry leaves on the flagstones!
It is like our bedroom from another summer,
The same bed, but with the shutters closed.

II

Et là, parmi les fleurs des champs, celles de cire
Ne sont pas les moins émouvantes, peintes clair
Comme le veut l'espérance qui rêve
Même où s'est effacé le souvenir.

Et l'incroyant, qui s'attarde auprès d'elles,
Prend lui aussi la coupelle de verre,
L'élève, irrépressiblement, devant l'image,
Y reproduit le miracle du feu,

Puis la pose, infinie, et reprend sa route,
Ayant aimé le signe, faute du sens.
Qu'est-ce dans cette flamme qui va noircir,
Se dit-il, quel est dans ma voix le mot qui manque?

Tout est si lumineux pourtant, quand la nuit tombe,
Pourquoi dans toute vie une arche est-elle
Plus basse, et l'eau qu'elle fascine plus violente
À se jeter sous la voûte sonore?

II

And there among the wild flowers, the wax ones
Are not the least touching, brightly painted
In the manner wished for by the hope that dreams
Even now, when its memories have faded.

And the unbeliever who lingers near them
In turn takes up the glass cupel,
And raises it, irresistibly, before the image,
Reproducing the miracle of the fire,

Then puts it down, infinite, and sets out once more,
Having loved the sign, for want of meaning.
What in this flame that soon will darken,
He wonders, what is this word that my voice does not know?

Everything seems so luminous, when night falls,
Why is there in every life a lower arch,
And why does the water that it beguiles
Throw itself, so violent, beneath its echoing vault?

III

Et quelle énigme un lieu, quand ainsi les choses
Sont presque l'évidence bien que la mort!
On croirait qu'il y a de l'être, tant la lumière
Peut diminuer sans cesser d'être vive.

Et c'est aussi comme ces bruits de voix
Que l'on entend le soir sur l'eau tranquille.
Ils vont plus vite que l'onde que fait la pierre,
On ne distingue plus le lointain du proche.

Qui parle là, si près de nous bien qu'invisible?
Qui marche là, dans l'éblouissement mais sans visage?
Ainsi venaient les dieux, jadis, à des enfants
Qui jettent des cailloux sur l'eau, quand la nuit tombe.

III

And what an enigma, a place, when things
Are both so evident and so full of death!
You would think that to be has meaning, so much
Can the light diminish without losing its brightness.

It is also like the sounds of voices
You hear at evening on the still water.
They move faster than the ripples made by a stone,
You cannot tell the far from the near.

Who is speaking there, so close to us, though invisible?
Who is walking there, faceless in the dazzle?
Just so, the gods, in former times, would come
To children throwing pebbles on the water at nightfall.

IV

Tu vas, ta main contre la barque touche l'eau.
Les rameurs n'ont plus de visage.
Au ciel, l'Ourse est passée dans des branches claires,
La robe de la Vierge s'est déchirée.

Ne sommes-nous qu'un arbre qui a pris feu
Dans la durée sans conscience de soi?
Frappe parfois la foudre contre des feuilles
Et la parole est braise, qui végète

Au coude de deux branches. Puis brûle l'arbre
Et un second peut-être. Mais le ciel
A son autre lumière. Et n'a pas cessé
Le cycle de l'indifférence de l'étoile.

IV

You go on, your hand against the boat touches the water.
The oarsmen are faceless now.
In the heavens, the Bear has moved over into bright branches,
The Virgin's robe is torn.

Are we but a tree that has caught fire
In time that does not know itself?
The lightning sometimes flashes among the leaves,
And speech is this burning ember that languishes

At the juncture of two branches. Then the tree burns,
Two trees, perhaps. But the sky
Has its own light. And the cycle
Of the star's indifference has not ceased.

V

Tu vas, et il te semble encore que s'élargit
Le fleuve de la lune sur les arbres.
Peut-être qu'une vie tressaille, dans le miroir
De la forêt qui reflète les mondes?

Mais non, astres et branches se confondent,
Et rêves et chemins. La nuit est une pierre
Qui barre étincelante le cours du fleuve.
À quatre heures déjà le jour se lève.

V

You go on, and once again it seems to you that
The moon's river has widened on the trees.
A life, perhaps, is stirring, in the mirror
Of the forest that reflects the worlds?

But no, branches and stars are mingling now,
As mingle paths and dreams. Night is a stone
That, gleaming, blocks the flow of the river.
By four o'clock, day is already rising.

La Barque aux deux sommeils

I

Glisse la barque étroite aux deux sommeils
Qui respirent l'un près de l'autre, sans recherche
De rien, dans l'immobilité, qu'un même souffle.
À l'aube le courant va plus rapide,
La barre qu'on n'entend pas de nuit gronde là-bas,
L'enfant qui joue à l'avant de la barque

Alors a compassion et se rapproche
Car ceux qui dorment là n'ont pas de visage,
Rien que ces deux flancs nus qui firent confiance
L'un à la joie de l'autre; et l'aube est froide,
L'eau sombre a des reflets d'une autre lumière.

Il s'approche, il se penche,
Il voit dans leur travail l'homme, la femme,
C'est une terre pauvre, dont les voies
Sont emplies d'eau comme après les orages.
Il place dans ce sol
Le germe d'une plante, qui recouvre
De ses palmes bientôt, sans souvenirs,
Le lieu de l'origine, aux rives basses.
C'est elle qu'il pressent, depuis déjà
Les premiers mots en lui, quand il regarde
Monter le soir ces piliers de fumée
Là-bas, loin dans la paix des deux branches du fleuve.

Et c'est elle qu'il veut, contre le ciel,
Voir croître chaque jour, dans l'évidence
Des oiseaux qui se croisent en criant.
Il ira tard le soir dans son feuillage,

The Boat of the Two Dreams

I

Over the waters glides the narrow boat, two dreamers
Breathing beside one another; they seek,
In the stillness, nothing but to be the same breath.
At dawn, the current flows more swiftly,
The shoal, which is inaudible at night,
Can now be heard grumbling somewhere down there,
The child playing at the prow of the boat

Takes pity then and comes closer,
For those sleeping near him are faceless,
Being only these two bare flanks that trusted
In each other's joy; and dawn is cold,
The dark water reflects another sky.

He draws near and bends down,
He sees the man, the woman, in the midst of their labor,
It is but a poor earth, whose paths
Are filled with water, as after storms.
He places in this ground
The seed of a plant that soon
Covers with its palms, memoryless,
The low-banked place where all things began.
He had sensed it, ever since
The very first words in him, as he watched
Those pillars of smoke rising at evening,
Down there, far off in the peacefulness
Of the two long branches of the river.

And now, it is what he wants to see growing
Each day against the sky in the bright clearness
Of the birds that cross each other, clamoring.
Late at evening, he will go among its leaves,

Il cherchera le fruit dans la couleur,
Il en pressera l'or dans ses mains paisibles,

Puis il prendra la barque, il ira poser
Le vin du temps désert, dans une jarre,
Au pied du dieu du rêve, agenouillé
Les yeux clos, souriant,
Dans les herbes lourdes de graines du bord du fleuve.

There he will seek the fruit in the color,
He will press its pure gold in his quiet hands,

Then he will take the boat, and he will go
To place this wine of empty Time, in a jar,
At the foot of the god of dreams, who kneels,
Smiling, his eyes closed,
In the seed-swollen grasses of the river bank.

II

Ils dorment. Fut vaincu enfin le temps qui œuvre
Contre toute confiance, toute joie.
Peut-être même que leur forme laisse sourdre
La lumière du rêve, qui ruisselle
Devant beaucoup des barques qui avancent
Avant le jour dans les pays de palmes.

Ils dorment. Et l'enfant revient à la proue,
Il contemple à nouveau, qui étincelle
Maintenant, l'eau du fleuve. Puis il rassemble
Des branches pour le feu, qu'il allume, serré
Dans un vase de terre. Et il s'endort,
Coloré par la flamme qui veille seule.

II

They are sleeping. Time, that works against
All confidence, and joy, has been vanquished.
Who knows? Perhaps their form allows the light
Of their dream to well up, this light that flows
Before so many of the boats that move
Forward, at break of day, in the land of palms.

They are sleeping. And the child returns to the prow,
Once again he looks at the river water,
Which is glistening now. Then he gathers
Branches for the fire, which he lights, packed
In an earthen vessel. And he goes to sleep,
Lit up by the flame that stands watch alone.

III

Ils rêvent. Dans la vie comme dans les images
C'est vrai que la valeur la plus claire avoisine
L'ombre noire de là où les mots se nouent
Dans la gorge de ceux qui ne savent dire
Pourquoi ils cherchent tant, dans le temps désert.

Ils vont. Et la couleur qui brasse la nuée
Prend parfois par hasard dans ses mains de sable
Leur désir le plus nu, leur guerre, leur regret
Le plus cruel, pour en faire l'immense
Château illuminé d'une autre rive.

III

They dream. In life, as in images,
The brightest spot is near the darker shadow,
Which is the place in words where words knot up
In the throats of those who can never say
Why they are searching so, in the deserts of time.

They go. And the color that stirs the cloud
Sometimes happens to take in its hands of sand
Their most naked desire, their war, their cruelest
Regret, to make of them the vast,
Illuminated castle of another shore.

IV

L'étoile dans la chose a reparu,
Elle en grossit le grain qui se fait moins trouble,
La grappe de ce qui est donne à nouveau
La joie simple de boire à ceux qui errent,
Les yeux emplis de quelque souvenir.

Et ils se disent que peu importe si la vigne
En grandissant a dissipé le lieu
Où fut rêvée jadis, et non sans cris
D'allégresse, la plante qu'on appelle
Bâtir, avoir un nom, naître, mourir.

Car ils pressent leurs lèvres à la saveur,
Ils savent qu'elle sourd même des ombres,
Ils vont, ils sont aveugles comme Dieu
Quand il prend dans ses mains le petit corps
Criant, qui vient de naître, toute vie.

Et tout alors, c'est comme un vase qui prend forme,
La couleur et le sable se sont unis.
Les mondes de l'imaginaire se dissipent.
Quelque chose s'ébauche qui ressemble
À des cailloux qui brillent dans l'eau claire.

IV

The star in things has reappeared,
It swells their grain which is less obscure,
The clusters of what is give once again
The simple joy of drinking to those who wander,
Their eyes filled with some memory.

And they tell themselves that it hardly matters
That the growing vines have scattered the place
Where once, and not without cries of joy,
They imagined the plant that people call
Building, having a name, coming to birth, dying.

For they press their lips to the savor of things,
They know that it wells up even from the shadows,
They go on, they are blind like God
When he takes in his hands the tiny, crying
Body that has just been born, all life.

And everything then is like a vase as it takes shape,
Color and sand are joined together.
The imaginary worlds are dispelled.
The outline of something takes form
That is like pebbles gleaming in clear water.

La Tâche d'Espérance

C'est l'aube. Et cette lampe a-t-elle donc fini
Ainsi sa tâche d'espérance, main posée
Dans le miroir embué sur la fièvre
De celui qui veillait, ne sachant pas mourir?

Mais il est vrai qu'il ne l'a pas éteinte,
Elle brûle pour lui, malgré le ciel.
Des mouettes crient leur âme à tes vitres givrées,
Ô dormeur des matins, barque d'un autre fleuve.

The Task of Hope

It is dawn. Has this lamp, then, finished
Its task of hope, hand placed
In the clouded mirror, on the fever
Of the one who kept watch, not knowing how to die?

But it is true that he has not put it out,
It still burns for him, in spite of the sky.
The seagulls screech their soul at your frost-covered
Window, morning sleeper, boat from another river.

Interview
with
Yves Bonnefoy

JOHN NAUGHTON: This book of poems was published twelve years after your last book of poetry, *Dans le leurre du seuil*. There are certain resemblances, at least superficially, between the two works: similar images, a "negative" voice that rises up once more, the evocation of the same house. What is the relation, in your eyes, between the two books? Or if you prefer, between this book and your previous work? How does the transition between one work and another come about? What is the meaning of the French title *Ce qui fut sans lumière* (*What Was without Light*)?

YVES BONNEFOY: Yes, there are a number of common elements in the two books. In the first place, I have never sought, or wanted, to forsake my beginnings, the traces in me of my childhood, the categories of thought that I have developed little by little over the course of time. These things can only be changed while one is in the process of writing books, not beforehand as a theoretical decision. Secondly, it is true that the pages you have translated are marked, all through the first part and beyond, by a place that has been the scene of my thoughts about hope, delusion, error, truth, ever since my book *Pierre écrite*, which appeared in 1965—the house at Valsaintes that I have spoken to you about so often, with all its connotations. These two elements have obviously created a bridge between the two books. And as a writer, I had never felt such continuity as strongly before. But I should also stress that this continuity became just as much for me the occasion, and the material, for a reassessment. As always when I begin a new book of poetry—and this because it's the only reason to start one—I saw that those memories, feelings, thoughts, and even those aspects of a place that is obviously a real place, were in fact an insufficient reading of what is; they were the language that breaks away from the world it should tell of, . . . a truth more imagined than truly lived, a light in which pools of shadow dwell beneath the rims of brightness. You mentioned a "negative" voice. It is

In October 1989, Yves Bonnefoy answered, in writing, a number of questions concerning *In the Shadow's Light* that were put to him by the translator, John Naughton.

the awareness that the presence of the world is withdrawing into the very words that seek to tell of it, and that there is therefore something "unthought of" in one's relation to oneself that feeds this negativity—and this explains the French title of the book: it recognizes what has remained an *otherness* in the *I* that had spoken.

JN: Should this book then be read as a kind of "revision"? As the elucidation of those aspects of the past that have remained in obscurity while others have been given an attention that is ultimately arbitrary, if not excessive?

YB: Yes, certainly, a revision. But I should perhaps try to specify as clearly as possible—even if this means having recourse to abstractions—the nature of this past, of this obscurity, that is being reconsidered. I don't agree with a number of contemporary critics who see poems merely as verbal constructions, as what simply activates and multiplies the relations that exist between words. I think, and in fact I have always thought, that poetry is an experience of what goes beyond words: call it the fleeting perception, then the more active remembrance, of a state of indifferentiation, of unity—that state that characterizes reality at the level that our language cannot reach, despite its definitions, its designations, and its descriptions. This unity deserves to be perceived by us, to be kept in mind, because in it the part becomes the whole, consciousness is no longer kept separate from it, and as a consequence, death ceases to be; it becomes simple metamorphosis, and so our anguish is quieted, and the soul and body are at peace with one another. But language has replaced this immediacy in our relation to the world with a system of representation which is nothing more than a partial view of it; it thus fragments this unity, drives it away, and so condemns us to exile and makes us fear death. And therefore, we would be lost if it weren't for poetry. Why poetry? Because by paying attention as it does to the sonorous part of words, to their capacity for rhythm, for music, poetry allows a relation to be established between words that is no longer simply the play of those abstract concepts that normally constitute our language. For a moment, the usual reading of the world, that network of figures which keeps Presence hidden, is neutralized, torn open; we stand before each thing as though before the entire universe, in an absolute that seems to welcome us. And this is why we write poems. Through them, we try to fix in our consciousness—it, too, formed by language—those moments that open to the intuition that all language refuses.

And thus there is something paradoxical about this undertaking, which strictly speaking is an impossibility, and which in any case needs to be constantly questioned, rescued from the language that takes form the moment writing begins: this dissatisfaction, this "negativity" being ultimately, through the rigorousness of the witness it bears, the poets' contribution to truth. Poetry is, from this point of view, the repudiation of poems. And it is precisely this kind of repudiation that I attempted in my way in *Ce qui fut sans lumière,* through the awareness of the contradictions and insufficiencies that mark my previous book, *Dans le leurre du seuil*—or at the very least that mark my relation to this work. How did the earlier book end? With a section called "The Scattered, the Indivisible," which allowed me to attest to Oneness, to the indivisibility of Being, in the very place where our language fragments it, where our illusions do violence to it; and in words, I had touched upon what seemed to me, in my own being, and for the future, a deliverance that would last. But this presence that was almost lived, this sacred order I had almost found in the very heart of daily things and in the ruins of dream, this too must have been only a dream, for my relation to what was the principal object of my attention at the time, to the major protagonist in my search for truth, did not evolve as it should have. The element I am referring to, the thing that had given me this opportunity for research, was my house at Valsaintes. In the beginning, I had made the place the material of a great dream, the dream of being able to live there, simply, in its atemporality and quiet transparency; I had spoken of it and loved it with the words of this dream. Then I was compelled to understand that the reality of this place was much more complex and contradictory than I had thought, that it escaped from my hold on it, that this entrance that it seemed to be into the "true life" was really a lure, an illusion; and thus I tried—this is the whole point of the earlier book—to learn from this example to sacrifice my desire, to love without having, in short, to rid myself of the dream, but in return to attain to that Oneness that exists beyond possessions and dreams—the illusion, understanding itself as such, becoming again a threshold. A beautiful thought, but more imagined and desired than truly lived. For, from that time forward, I should have forgotten, if not the house, at least my desire to live in it, to suit it to my life in the way I had thought possible in the beginning and for a long time afterwards. But in place of this, I was seized once more by the old longings that had rekindled in me; I imagined myself once more in the old site, in the empty rooms; I rejected once again the thought of all the insoluble difficulties associated with living there. And so I dreamed—even at night, even in the depths of sleep—as I had done on the first days so long ago. "Ce souvenir me hante"—"I am haunted by this memory"—these, then, are the very first words of *Ce qui fut sans lumière*.

JN: Could you tell us a little bit about this house at Valsaintes which occupies so central a place in all your poetry of the last twenty-five years? It once was a monastery, wasn't it? Where is it exactly? When and how did you find it? How do you explain its importance in your life, and more generally speaking, how is it that a place can come to play so significant a role in an existence? What is your present relation to this house? How do you feel about it today?

YB: It was by chance, yes, truly by chance, in the summer of 1963, that we came into a part of Haute-Provence in the south of France which was, and still is, rather deserted, and which seems cut off from the world. Wooded hills, a vast sky, narrow paths that run among the stones beneath the red clouds, the eternity of the simple rural life, the few shepherds, the flocks of sheep, silence everywhere: only Virgil or Poussin, whom I loved so much, had spoken to me seriously of these things, and this by means of what is most secret and intimate in their work: the mystery of the most fundamental and unembellished architectural forms, certainly, but more still the stirring of a shadow on words engraved in stone, or the distant sound of cattle-bells. We wanted to live here, and we went everywhere in search of a house, and then a few days later, at the end of a road that wasn't on the map, that didn't even seem to fit in with what we knew at the time about the general structure of the places around there, there was a tremendous storm, rain that suddenly became a deluge and into which we had nevertheless to throw ourselves: and in the midst of the black mass of water, long walls suddenly appeared, with low, vaulted doors, that disappeared on all sides beneath the heavy downpour. We went in; it was almost night inside, and we visited a labyrinth of rooms without understanding what they were, rooms in which dry hay that seemed to have been brought in many years before was piled up against pillars, under paintings. In fact, we were in a nave, in a chancel, then in chapels, although there was a staircase running crosswise and huge lofts above. We wandered there amid the clamoring of birds we had disturbed and the sounds of the wind against the tiles that were coming apart; then we went out into the last rays of the evening sun that had reappeared and found ourselves in front of the slopes and terraces of a ravine in which almond trees were mingled with oaks. And among them, we even found to our delight that there were some olive trees, which you would not have seen any further north because of the colder winters there. This was the beginning of several years of profound attachment, despite great difficulties, and even a sense of contradiction that was painful to experience. We got rid of the hay and the partitions that the peasants had added after the Revolution to reduce the size of the rooms, and thus, thanks to our efforts, the religious character of what once had been the church was restored, but its authority scarcely lent itself to the daily life we had to lead, even though we tried—in vain of course—to bring this life as close as possible to the being of the snake beneath the stones of the entrance, or the buzzards and the owls and the hoopoes that built their nests in the walls or in the open barns. There was more of the real here than anywhere else, more immanence in the light on the angle of the walls or in the water from new storms, but there were also a thousand forms of impossibility—I won't go into all the turns this took for want of time—and so there was also more dreaming. And the year came when we had to shut the place up, give it back to the silence of before. Only the birds live there now; they come in and out of one or two broken windows with loud cries. Except for the shadows—and here you will recognize the first pages of the book—that memory delegates through dreams to the places it loves. At night these shadows renew the life of summers past, the life that, all in all, engendered some happiness and meaning for awhile.

JN: In *Ce qui fut sans lumière,* there is not only the meditation on the importance of the moments spent in the house at Valsaintes, there is also the evocation of an even more distant past, of childhood. Is there a relation between the recent and the more distant past? Does the memory of the one call forth thoughts about the other? How does the relation between the two affect the structuring of your book?

YB: There is no doubt that the house at Valsaintes had such a powerful attraction for me because, being at one and the same time a church and a granary—a monastery and a place where sheep and goats still made their home—it seemed to suggest a fusion of those things that speak of the divine and forms of daily existence, a fusion adding resonance and intensity to the surrounding countryside, which, in those days, was still completely given over to the spell of the eternal. But when, in a certain place, immanence and transcendence are able to become the same sound of cattle-bells, the same colored sandstone, when the moss seems a kind of unknown writing, this can also recall—and it's obviously an important connection—one's earliest childhood, those years when the child, who as yet has hardly learned to speak and is still on the threshold of those words which will fragment the unity of being, lives enveloped in the eternity a mother provides. I believe that Valsaintes revived and nourished my old Oedipal nostalgia, that its power derived from that first, all-important proof of it, which its high walls, its colors in the evening, its breathing at night seemed to be, and that I was therefore led to think that I had at last found the place that I had desired for so long—the kind of place I talk about in my book *L'Arrière-pays*—and the kind of natural, elementary time that is untouched by the degradation of the absolute that clocks subject us to. And there is, indeed, in these certainly unusual impressions, enough to waken in the person who is moved in this way the most deeply buried words, the oldest memories, and those aspirations that are the most radically previous to everything suggested by the culture learned later—and therefore enough to stir up this person's relation to words, his poetry, as hands that plunge into a puddle stir up the sleeping darkness and mingle mud and light.

And this was not a simple delusion. For Valsaintes gave me back, if not the garden of Eden, at least something of the way in which the child looks at the world. And the house—which reminded me, moreover, of another one, where I had spent the summers of my youth—led me perhaps to think seriously about childhood, and better understand the meaning of this period in the structure of life, and vaguely foresee the ways in which it might be capable of solving the problems of adult, or modern, consciousness—a capacity which is not acknowledged today. As you know, a child is the central figure in *Dans le leurre du seuil;* he dwells in the tree of that book, an almond tree, a real one, and it was this child that helped me to chase away illusions and get the better of what might have trapped me: the one who has the absolute in his eyes both looks into our dream and sees higher and further. And thanks to the child, and despite so many ambiguities, that strange and so simply real mass of stone, that house that was like a second birthplace, had a very positive value for me when all is said and done, despite those nightly returnings I mentioned a moment ago, the ones that continued to pursue the illusion that Valsaintes was the "true place," the one and only true place above the world.

JN: You have divided this book, as you have all your other books, into sections—and in this case, into five parts. How do you explain the structure of the book? What is the relation between the various sections? How do you write these sections? Do you write them one after another, or do they come to you all at once? Do you write the individual poems with some sequence in mind, or does the idea of a structure come later, and with it the sense of the place for each of the various texts?

YB: I think we have to make a distinction between the surface structures and the deeper structures. The former are forms of writing; they develop in the book as so many aspects of its text and can be seen, for instance, in its successive parts—or, more accurately, its simultaneous parts, since the sequences in a book of poetry only seem to come one after another; in fact, they are born together in a verbal space where even the slightest decision needs to see and know—whether consciously or not—everything about what determines the author in his situation at the moment. Here and there, in the process of writing, clusters of words or sentences emerge, of course, that seem to precede others, but these are still, in my case at least, unfinished pages, pages that, in order to crystallize, need the contribution of other such emerging clusters, whose presence gives them new meaning; and thus four or five cardinal points take shape in the space of words—four if one follows the teaching of the simple earthly horizon, five if one remembers, along with Henri Corbin and a whole mystical tradition, that, on the paths we follow, in addition to the four sides of the sky, there is also the star of a deep north, of an orient, that transcends or at least blurs them. . . .

But the deeper structure is something entirely different. This is the structure of the forces that are in us, whether we write or not, the structure of the experiences that we have had and that guide us or lead us astray—the conflict that we are, beyond the reconciliation and equilibrium that writing sometimes manages to produce. And in this new book, *Ce qui fut sans lumière,* I think that, from this point of view, I can recognize the presence, the influx, of two situations, of two moments in my life: on the one hand, the house at Valsaintes, which had become a simple memory, but which still tormented me in my moments of insomnia and longing, and, on the other hand, experiences and a place, which I'll tell you about in a moment, that are certainly the very opposite of that inextricable knot of illusions and promises. . . . Two poles, and between the two, a field of forces that this time are not simple elements in the writing of the book, since they are situated on a level where it is the very need to write, in order to understand these forces, that has to take shape once more, in the midst of new signifiers. The opposition between the two experiences, the discordant effects, will be the given of the book, not the work it accomplishes, nor the form it will take on in the process of this work. I mentioned "surface" structures: these are what will carry, differentiate, connect, the thoughts that are born from the deeper tension—and these are also what will try to dissipate this tension, by better understanding its contradictory lessons. To write poetry means thinking, but through form, through music—music which helps, if we know how to listen. Poetry is what tries to make music of what occurs in life.

JN: This brings us to the idea of a "narrative" which, although it is extremely discrete—almost completely hidden—gives a certain form to your book. In fact, I think that it could be argued that a deeply buried narrative line runs through all of your books of poetry. How do you see the relation between lyrical expression and the organization of an ensemble of these expressions in a certain narrative order? You'll see that I'm still fascinated by the question of how your books become structured.

YB: Yes. The very fact that poetry is the effort to give meaning to life, and to what it holds in store, is the proof that there are already facts beneath its words, facts with which one could develop a story, however unlike a novel this story might appear—for these are very ordinary things, those which give meaning to our lives. There are events, past or virtual, hidden in the depths of a poem, and even if they are not made explicit, many of their elements are nonetheless visible in brief evocations which provide writing with its metaphors, or, through a fleeting metonymy, enrich the great symbols that are in all poetry and already active in the author's mind. And it is very fortunate that this is so, for now the ship of words, which is so apt to go off in any direction, is anchored in things, and facts, that exceed the imaginary.

In the case of *Ce qui fut sans lumière,* the second pole—that is, as I said, the other place, the other lesson—was for me the forest between Massachusetts and Vermont, and the snow in the light there. At this point I should tell you that I have always seen the earth, in its various aspects and also in the diverse responses that the work of civilization has inscribed in it, as a variety of propositions about existence, almost all of which speak to me, some with particular power, and in this latter case, there was a similar intensity for me. More precisely, the appeal of the Mediterranean site, that seems to offer the possibility of bringing together the essential things of life in a simple, obvious form, a figure of the absolute as immediately perceptible and inexhaustible as a circle traced in stone on a classical facade—think of Alberti, of Piero della Francesca—is countered in me by the light of Northern Europe, which passes through moments of darkness when the rain falls, but which comes out again a moment later all the more brilliant and joyful, and so speaks of hope: remember those sudden and ephemeral "spells of light" that are so glorious and miraculous in the Irish skies, or think of Constable's paintings. And the United States has always attracted me because of the immensity of the space that opens up before the traveler, and because of the long roads there that seem snatched up by the infinite even before the horizon: lessons in decentering that teach us that we are nothing but a fleeting shadow on the earth.

Now it happens that I was especially sensitive to this second kind of lesson in 1985, in New England, where I spent several months at Williamstown. I would walk in Hopkins Forest, which at first was green and then full of color in autumn and finally grey and black, but lit up by the snow. At nightfall I would watch the lights of the cars fleeing silently along a road on a distant hillside beyond the woods—they seemed to me to be headed for someplace beyond the world. Sheets of snow were here and there and everywhere, and the quickly fading rust of the trees stood out against the whiteness, thus fragmenting the physical world and making the distances seem greater. It was as though the far away were already begun here, and the cred-ibility of this place of life was thus affected, and yet, on the roads or in the streets of the village, nothing was more joyous than the flakes of snow that swirled in the bracing air, making the colors brighter and soon giving place to skies that seemed bluer— though without vehemence—than any summer sky can be. Here was the way to give up possessions, if one were capable of it, and even to free oneself from those images, such as Val-saintes, that are also possessions when one believes in them, since they guarantee certainties. And all of this came at just the right time, given the disappointments and the decisions—and also the relapses—that I spoke about. I tried to listen to the lesson, perhaps without great success—the future will tell—but this is then the other pole in *Ce qui fut sans lumière*. What is its relation to the writing of poetry, you ask? One might call it the salt that, in the alembic of writing, allows for transmutations. Or, while we wait for them to occur, the source of images that allow us to anticipate them.

JN: Dreams seem to play an important role in this book. In your experience, what is the relation between dreams and poetic inspiration?

YB: Why dreams, why give them such importance? It is because writing, and even speaking, in the most ordinary sense of the word, means dreaming, since the language that writing and speaking employs, and also produces, and that seems to open onto action, gives only a simple image of reality, an image drawn in broad strokes by our desires. The discourse of the

"man of action"—the politician, for instance—is as much con-
stituted by the imaginary as the writer's is; it is in fact even more
illusory since it does not recognize itself as such. It would have
us believe that we are perfectly awake, and because of this illu-
sion or lie, not only the experience of Oneness but also the inner
world of the psyche become inaccessible, hidden as they now
are by these partial representations that have been abstracted
from nature or existence. And in these conditions, dreaming,
free dreaming, the kind that is never really able to believe—even
if it wanted to—that it is reality, is a duty as much as a danger,
and this is true for poetry as well. In other words, it is the ac
tivity that—overflowing the confines of the impoverished
illusions, freeing desire from its entrapment in stereotypical ob-
jects, refusing the constraints, the resignation that compensate,
through violence, a deep frustration and anguish—keeps life in
contact with the intensity one senses in it: an intensity which,
when it is fully taken on and understood, could find satisfaction
in the simplest things the world proposes. Is not the imaginary
the trouble suffered by those who allow themselves to be pris-
oners of a language that is closed—of ideologies, of desires be-
come fantastical? Dreaming, in poetry, is to stop dreaming.

JN: Your book is marked by a whole network of signs that speak
both of beginnings and endings, anguish and joy, disappoint-
ment and resurgent hope, and in such a way as to suggest that
for you these things are inseparable, that what seems to be in
opposition is in fact a single truth about life. How do you see
these juxtapositions, these things that appear to be the antith-
esis of one another but that you present as somehow one? And
how does the idea of reconciling these contradictory realities
influence the question of composition, of structuring, we were
discussing a moment ago?

YB: Those juxtapositions, or rather even that identity of opposites,
those oxymorons that no longer are a simple playing with
words—like the "icy fires" of the rhetoric of preciosity—but
rather experiences that one lives? Well, this would be the "true
life." For if you open yourself to the One, there is no more

death. You are all things; and the outer becomes the inner, the ephemeral the eternal, and absolute dispossession is the supreme richness. But who knows how to live like this? Language deprives us of that closeness to the world we need, and in fact, it is language that institutes those oppositions which are nothing but a partial view of things. And so all that remains to poetry is the resource of making of the oxymoron one of the ways of remembering what is beyond language, and perhaps even of drawing a little closer to this through rough sketches of experimentations that can only have meaning as a disruption of logic—logic, that exile from Being. The fusion of opposites is the star that guides poetry—even if beginnings and endings, as you say, or anguish and joy, can never do more, in poetry, than draw near to one another, then quickly separate, although they may flutter together for a moment like two flakes of snow in the light.

JN: The visual arts have a central place in your life. You have written dozens of essays on the arts and on various artists from Piero and Poussin to contemporary figures such as Miró, Giacometti, and Hopper. Many of your closest friends are painters. And the visual arts have also inspired some of your own poetry and your thoughts about poetry as a genre of expression. You have often taken specific works of art as subjects for your poems. In *Ce qui fut sans lumière,* there are two poems devoted to works of art: the text on Claude Lorrain's *Landscape with Psyche and the Palace of Amor* and the long poem on Constable's painting *Dedham from Langham.* How do these evocations of works of art fit into the overall scheme of the book? How do they contribute to its major preoccupations? And, more generally speaking, how do you see the relation between poetry and painting? How does the one become a commentary on the other?

YB: We want to be in the world, don't we? We want to simplify desire so that it might be as universal, as transparent, as the thirst that fresh water satisfies. This is why painting matters to poetry.

It's true that painters are almost as much prisoners of words as poets are. Isn't the world they look at also structured by language? But painters can perceive directly, fully perhaps, the pure sensory quality that is denied to language, that is beyond the word in things; thus they see color, which has no meaning, lines whose quivering says more than the very figures they delimit. And because of this, they can drink from what-is in a way the poet never can, and what an example they therefore become for him, and what nostalgia, what incitement they provide! Painters can seem to be the water you are looking for when you are thirsty. Remember Rimbaud: he too made *thirst* a metaphor for the desire for being, and in his poem "Larme," he depicts himself bending over the water of a stream but not being able to drink. But we also see him looking at the storm paintings in the sky, at their black tones, their reds, their blues that a painter has the power to recreate on his canvas. The painter leads us in our approach to immediacy beyond the point where language stops.

It is nonetheless true that a great many painters have also let themselves be captivated, like the poets, by the fantastic representations that words can substitute for the simple reality of the world, and the distinction that I have just made—in terms altogether too broad—between poetry and painting, can also be applied to painting itself, which allows poets to recognize in some painters a reflection of their own cause, as Hamlet said of Laertes, and the sufferings of a similar exile. In his poem "Les Phares," Baudelaire brought together a number of the great names of the "poetic tradition" that exists in painting. He needed to go by way of what Delacroix, who was perhaps the only representative of true romantic poetry in France, had seen, in order to reach what Delacroix had all the same attained to despite his dreaming and his sorrows: that is, the green of the meadows, the fires of the setting sun.

And it is something like the same need that explains why Constable and Claude Lorrain are brought together in *Ce qui fut sans lumière*. I think of Constable as one of those who have gone the furthest towards the fullness, the completeness, the infinite simplicity the world offers—how can I say it?—at certain moments when consciousness seems freed from language. The Zen painters would have loved him. But he is also one who sees Dedham "from Langham"—that is to say, from another, faraway place, which turns the object of vision into something mysterious, into something that is not desired in the ordinary way, that is already almost a form of transcendence, a dream, already the inscription of the illusory in painting. And from the outset, Claude Lorrain is obviously the painter of those "Dedhams" on the shores beyond the sea, of those harbors with "vast porticoes," that seem to be the absolute established in peace in this world. But he also painted *Psyche and the Palace of Amor*, which is a profound analysis of the mirages created by distance, of the melancholy that comes from idle dreaming, of the way in which the soul lost in dreams can become alienated from love. And so, these evocations of paintings in my book are meant to signify the ever-recurring conflicts in speech between representation, which is always illusory, and presence, which is always furtive. The painted image permits us a spectrum analysis of what takes place in writing: it is the convex mirror in which writing can take full stock of itself, recognize what it is, and think about its problem.

JN: Speaking of images, how is one to understand your own poetic images—the ones that recur throughout the book: the image of a boat, for instance, or the image of the child who seems to guide consciousness toward an unknown future, or the image of paths that close?

YB: I can speak about poetry in general, since this transcends personal factors, and I can speak about the conditions in which I write, since these go beyond the actual writing. But writing, from the outset, is a subversion of ordinary meanings, an interaction in the words between intentions and effects, a great many of which are unconscious, a deployment of symbols that think as if by themselves without the writer who works with them knowing exactly what he is saying through them, and I therefore couldn't speak with any authority about anything whatsoever that concerns the text itself of my poems. Why that boat, why the child who appears in *Le Pays du sommet des arbres* or *L'Agitation du rêve?* Perhaps you know better than I, since you can see me from the side, from behind, standing, bent over, whereas I have only a frontal view of myself. Let me put it another way: of course when I write I have intentions, conceptions, elaborations that sometimes are even far too complex. But these nets are ceaselessly crossed and pierced by darting black forms that right away regain the depths. And so I too seek to know the meaning of that boat that came over from *Dans le leurre du seuil,* and thus I give movement to it: sometimes it is the barque of the dead of ancient cultures; sometimes it is a little boat stopped in the middle of the river under the sky and so an image of the peacefulness of the mind in the sufficiency of the moment. But these are only some aspects among others, aspects I haven't controlled, and in order to know more, I have to write again and search, but in ways that have nothing to do with critical thinking. I have to go under the cover of words and be amid their sounds that are like foliage, like tree trunks crowded together, and between them the path never ceases to vanish.

JN: Readers of your poetry have often called attention to what seems to be a certain contradiction: you aspire to immediacy, to transparency, but you sometimes evoke these by means of references to works of art or to philosophical categories. In short, you speak of the importance of an unmediated simplicity through a cultural mediation. And there can be no doubt that allusions to the monuments of our culture abound in your work. In *Ce qui fut sans lumière,* there are the evocations of the paintings we discussed a moment ago, but there are also quotations from John Donne, allusions to Hegel, to the *Egyptian Book of the Dead,* to Dante, and so forth. How do you yourself see this contradiction, if, in fact, there is a contradiction?

YB: Most of the allusions that you mention do not figure in what, strictly speaking, is my poetic text, but rather are a part of the thought that accompanies it—although often so closely, it's true, as to seem one with it. The titles or the epigraphs placed at the beginning of the books are reflections of this sort. In the poems themselves, on the other hand, I refer almost always to things of nature or places lived in. But we must not forget that the space of existence has aspects that derive from culture. Shakespeare or Dante are a part of it as well as the house at Valsaintes, which itself is full of signs—I mentioned some of these a moment ago—that speak of its past, or of the hopes and the precepts of a religious tradition. And it is also true that certain of these "cultural" aspects of our relation to ourselves possess something that makes of them—and this is important for me— the mirror that reflects not so much the image, and not the thing, as the absolute that we look for in the latter. As we move in search of Oneness, *The Winter's Tale*, for instance, is not more exterior than the tree or the stone, since what we see made available to us in the play is that springtime intoxication through which men and women of the middle ages knew how to give themselves to life, at the end of a winter—an end which, tomorrow, could mean conceptual thought agreeing to share its power. Why shouldn't such works remain close to us when we work on poems? When we refer to them, it is as though our own speech, which we try to give to simple behavior, reached out to their luminous words and received from them an influx that encourages us to go forward.

JN: People who read *Ce qui fut sans lumière* might wonder about what comes next, might ask themselves if this book will be "continued" in future works of poetry—although the future, in *Ce qui fut sans lumière,* is presented as anything but clear. Are you working on poems at the present moment? To the extent that you try to imagine it, how do you envision your future work?

YB: Other attempts, yes, and forever. Since the word is so much more, in poetry, than the text in which language imprisons it, since it is—if I may so put it—the hostage of the text, how could one not want to go beyond the present text in the "openness" of that speech which has value precisely because it has not as yet found form? Each time that some light in the sky, or some important moment in life, speaks to us of the absolute—at every "spell of light" between the clouds of our inner North— the need for this poetic speech thrusts its claws into our spirit, and then there is nostalgia, but also a real hopefulness, for this impossible speech truly *is*, at that moment; it is like the ray of light that precedes dawn. And so I dream of "continuations" that might be transfigurations—absolutely unexpected, miraculous—even if I sometimes put off until later, much later, the moment of trying, because I know how many fallen branches and dry leaves must be picked up for there to be a chance of fire. But what can we say in advance, since the actual work is so often the discarding of its project? I shall simply say that after *Ce qui fut sans lumière,* I felt the need to write a few more poems on the subject, and in the brightness, of the snow—that is, based once again on my memories of New England. I call this small collection of poems *Début et fin de la neige.* But I have also written some prose-poems, one of which is about a child who gets lost, or who plays at getting lost, in the woods. And what I see ahead of me—and I think I can say this without risk of error—is a debate, in my writing, between poetry in verse and a kind of prose writing that is like neither usual narrative prose, nor the prose of an essay, but rather is the freedom of poetry once more, but this time released, at least at moments, from the constraints of prosody. In verse, music fills all the cords of the text with its vibrations. Nothing remains therefore except what has opened to it and submitted to its laws and thus is either clarified, since music is the Oneness that is felt in multiplicity, or remains there, still closed, still opaque, and yet wrapped in the brightness, which becomes a risk—the risk of perhaps forgetting to try to understand, to try to find a place in meaning for those parts of our speech that are thus like the blocks of ice in winter water that are sometimes barely visible. A risk, and perhaps as a consequence of it, the need for the prose-poem. When our attention to the musical side of speech is suspended for a moment, we can reestablish contact with those other dimensions which had not been able to find their place in the music and try to delve into their as yet unexplored depths.

JN: You are yourself a master translator. You have translated most of the tragedies of Shakespeare, as well as texts of Donne, Keats, Yeats, and others. Could you tell us a bit about this experience?

Can a work of poetry be translated without betraying it? Have you ever been tempted to translate your French texts into English yourself?

YB: Translating poetry,—I have given a great deal of thought to this paradoxical, disappointing, and exalting act that is as difficult as it is necessary, and I have written about it on many occasions. Just a word, then, for today. To go from one language to another, to reinvent in French the rhythms, the timbre, the vast areas of denotation and connotation in words that are the very terrain of poetic invention in Shakespeare or Yeats is obviously impossible. You cannot recreate on the piano all the sonorities, all the modulations, of the violin or the flute. But musicians know how to transpose to one instrument works that were written for another, or even for the whole orchestra, and it is true that whether on the violin, the flute, or the piano, each time it's still music, the soul of which is a harmony that is almost beyond the material element in sounds. Does this comparison have any applicability for us as translators? It certainly seems so to me, John, when I read what your piano has gotten from my violin, or from my little flute. I have sometimes felt that what is the most difficult to hear in a French poem is precisely what should be immediately perceptible to the ear, that is to say, the prosodic quality of the text. Our long and short syllables, the light and mobile accentuations that wander over the surface of the words according to the meaning or the form of the whole line, this is what escapes, even in France, readers who have not made poetry their life, their most intimate relation to language—literally their very breathing. And this is why I once tried myself to translate one of the sections of *Dans le leurre du seuil* into English. Since I was doing the translating myself, I thought that perhaps, beneath the awkwardness and the strangeness of my overly bookish English, something of the rhythm I feel without ever being able to explain it, except through direct practice, might appear. But you are hardly the one who needs such examples, and it may even be that your work now makes this experiment unnecessary.

Translated by John Naughton